A GUIDE TO THE REALES ALCAZARES IN SEVILLE

I. PREFACE

Los Reales Alcázares in Seville undoubtedly occupies a very outstanding place amongst the most beautiful palaces belonging to the Crown of Spain. It is a very intricate complex of areas and buildings where the passage of time and of history has left its sheen and its mark by weaving a rich tapestry of traditions and legends.

Its origins can be traced back as far as the 10C, but the Early Middle Ages and, after that, the Renaissance and the Baroque are the periods which formed and gave a distinguished air to this unique building in the very heart of the city of Seville. But, despite its age, the *Alcázar* or fortress is not an archaeological site because it has remained faithful to its original function as a Royal House, as a dwelling of the King. This means that even today it still serves its ancient purpose as a palace, a feature on which its vitality is based. The upper storey is in fact used by the Spanish monarch and his retinue when they visit Seville. The rooms of the upper *Cuarto Real* (= Royal Suite) were therefore closed to the public for a long time. As from now onwards, however, the Royal Trust is planning to open them to visitors also.

Whatever the case, the huge complex of buildings, the construction of which was begun in the late Middle Ages, has been lived in without interruption and until today it has undergone changes forced upon it by the needs and circumstances accompanying each of the moments in its long, chequered existence. The result is today's layout which –despite successive construction and destruction, one on top of the next– is still harmonious and balanced, full of beauty and charm, surprising and at the same time serene: in one word, a world of contrasts which is sometimes difficult to describe since it is essential it be felt and admired.

The high walls of the buildings and gardens forever enclose and guard stories and legends, but also facts and truths that were and still are fundamental milestones in the memory of this beloved country, which is Spain. Let us only remember personalities such as Al-Mutamid or King Don Pedro, who rebuilt this palace complex; or Alfonso X *el Sabio* (= the Wise) who found the inspiration there to write his *Cantigas* (= songs, ballads); or Queen Isabel who, behind these walls, founded the *Casa de la Contratación de las Indias*, a Chamber of Commerce for America, where many famous expeditions to the New World were organized and where she received Columbus after his return from his second voyage; or the Emperor Carlos who married the *Infanta Doña Isabel* of Portugal inviting personalities of the standing of Baldassare Castiglione, Garcilaso de la Vega or Boscán. In one word, there is an endless list of facts and people that will remain unmentioned, but that are proof of the enormous historical interest in this unique building.

For this reason the attraction of and the interest in *Los Reales Alcázares* in Seville are rather outstanding not only for historians and intellectuals in general, but for all kinds of visitors who enter the rooms and walk through the gardens. Recent research has made it possible to uncover countless new facts enlarging on and rounding off many aspects of this universally known building complex, which became part of the World Heritage in 1988. It is the aim of the present Guide to the *Reales Alcázares* in Seville to give publicity to the new findings and update what is known today. At the same time, by establishing the most appropriate itinerary for a visit of the architecture and gardens, it is meant to improve the understanding of and admiration for this impressive building, which is the most important of civil architecture in Seville.

II. ORIGINS OF THE *ALCAZAR*, A GENERAL OUTLINE OF THE HISTORICAL BACKGROUND AND THE MAIN ALTERATIONS MADE IN THE COURSE OF CENTURIES

From Roman times the area occupied by *Los Reales Alcázares* belonged to a very busy part outside the city. Close by there was the harbour area and the shops connected with the river traffic. The boundaries of this part were the River Guadalquivir, the Tagarete stream, the *Vía Augusta* and the curtain walls of the city.

There is proof that a palaeo-Christian basilica consecrated to St Vincent, Martyr, and including a baptistry stood on the site in the 5C. *San Isidoro* preached and was buried there and *San Leandro* with his disciples worked in it. The remains of this construction were found in the

Patio de Banderas (= Inner Court of Flags) (plate 2) and excavated in 1976. It appears that the basilica stood in a small acropolis surrounded by a walled enclosure and must have been in use until 844 when it was razed to the ground.

In 711 the Arabs conquered the peninsula and the city grew, spreading beyond the walls. It was further enlarged when it became the Islamic capital of *Al-Andalus* (= the Arabic name for Andalusia) a few years later. In the reign of Abd al-Rahman III (in 844) the Normans invaded and razed a large part of the city outside the walls. A series of repair works were undertaken after the invaders had been defeated.

2. Patio de Banderas

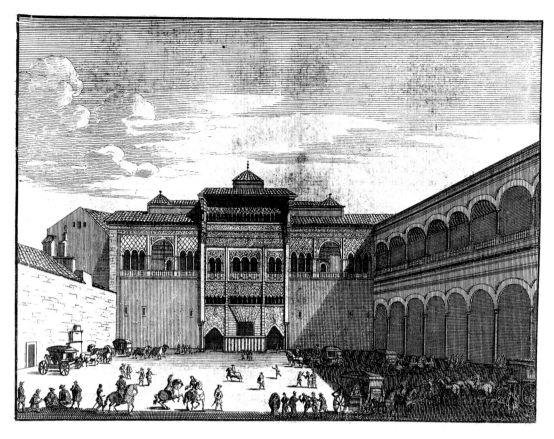

3. *Patio de la Montería.* (An etching)

According to Ibn al-Quttiya, it was in the course of these works when Abd al-Rahman III ordered the *Dar al-Imara*, the House of the Governor, to be built on the site of the former St Vincent Basilica. This house is the original centre of the *Alcázar* and dates from the first years of the 10C (913-914). It was built by Abdallah ben Sinan, a Syrian, and was a small fortress, the parade ground of which is today's *Patio de Banderas*, while the stony surface of the walls, which have survived to the present, faces today's *El Triunfo Square.* The original gate, which is walled up today, is also preserved in *Joaquín Romero Murube St.*

Thus the boundaries of this enclosure were today's *Santa Cruz* area and the *Patio de la Montería* (plate 3) and it probably stood isolated from the city. This is where the Banu Hachach and the Banu Abbad, great lords of the city, used to live as did the Kings Al-Mutadid and Al-Mutamid, important members of the latter dynasty.

During the reign of these two monarchs in the 11C, it became necessary to enlarge the original buildings since they were no longer big enough for the needs of the complex palace organization of the time. Consequently, the old fortress was enlarged towards the west, ie, the area of today's *Puerta de Jerez,* by adding a series of curtain walls. This new palace was called *Alcázar al-Muwarak* (= Fortress of the Benediction) and its main gate was next to the river. From there strong walls on either side accompanied the path which climbed up today's *Santander St* and *Miguel de Mañara St* and ended at a gate at the back, which gave direct access to the *Patio del León,* which used to be and still is a small area in front of the palaces. The 11C remains of this new building complex are preserved in the part of *La Contratación Square,* where the Royal House used to stand surrounded by a *patio* or inner court and a garden in the form of a cross. This is where the *Casa de la Contratación de las Indias* stood in the 16C.

The main hall of this palace was known by the name of Al-Turayya which means Hall of the Pleiades. It was a large square pavilion roofed with a dome and was used as the Throne Hall by the Banu Abbad King. Today it is identified with the *Salón de Embajadores* (= Ambassadors' Room) preserving all the alterations from the Mudéjar period. The *Sala de las Pléyades* was the meeting place of literary circles over which Al-Mutamid himself presided. He is said to have been the first poet of the *taifas,* the Spanish petty kingdoms.

The second important period for the *Alcázar* as regards alterations was the Almohad government (1147-1237) when Seville became the capital of the new empire. Abu Yaqub-Yusuf had the interior and exterior *Alcazabas* (= fortresses) built. The former is the area between the curtain walls of the city and the Alcázar, which was joined by the new walls from the riverside and by others, the remains of which are found inside Santa Marta Convent. There the main mosque was built with *La Giralda* towering over it.

In the same period a new military enclosure was built towards the south. It was a large triangular area encircled by a new wall which linked up with the original wall of *Dar al-Imara*, ie, with that of the *Patio de Banderas*, then formed an angle at the Tagarete stream and continued on its way. From time immemorial the area, which has just been described, has been called *Pradera de la Plata* (= Silver Meadow) and with the passage of time it would turn into the interior orchard and gardens of the *Alcázar* (plate 4). The centre would be an oratory in the form of a *cubba*, ie, a square ground plan covered with a dome. The enclosure was named after the chapel and became known as the *Huerta de la Alcoba* (= Orchard of the Bedroom).

4. A general view of the gardens

Near the river, there used to be another enclosure which was raised by the *almojarife*[0] Abu Hafs and must be identified with the site where *La Casa de la Moneda* (= the Mint) was later built and stood attached to the curtain walls of the city and to a wall of Al-Muwarak's Palace. In the area closest to the river, this enclosure included the *Cicca* or Muslim Mint, in the vicinity of which stood *La Torre de la Plata* (= Silver Tower) at one of the angles. Afterwards (1220 or 1221) a double wall was raised at this point and ended at *La Torre del Oro* (= Tower of Gold), the bow of the *Alcázar's* cutwater jutting out over the Guadalquivir.

In the same period this palace was rebuilt in the part between the Santa Cruz area and the *Patio de la Montería del Alcázar*, ie, the area originally occupied by the old *Dar al-Imara*.

It was to be the official residence of the Almohad monarchs with below, in the form of a cross, a lovely garden which would later be called *Baños de Doña María de Padilla* (= Doña María de Padilla's Baths) (plate 5).

5. Garden of *El Crucero* or Bath of *Doña María de Padilla*

Near this area there is also a beautiful, interesting *patio,* which is called *El Yeso (= Plaster),* because of the rooms and arcades surrounding it and their plaster decoration designed in a way considered totally novel and unique. Its portico was the source of inspiration for later Andalusian, especially Nasrid, architecture (plate 6).

In Al-Muwarak's enclosure, the Almohads also built another garden in the form of a cross and refurbished the rooms of the domestic Palace.

---

(0) Hist.: an official who collected the King's taxes and acted as the treasurer.

6. *Patio del Yeso*

7. *San Fernando.* Valdés Leal. (Detail). Catedral. Jaén

It was his son Alfonso *el Sabio* (= the Wise) (plate 8), who made some important alterations in order to adapt these Islamic buildings to the different needs of his Court. Thus in the middle of the 13C he rebuilt the old Almohad palace in a simple, modest fashion using the Gothic style. This palace stands above the cross-shaped garden in the original enclosure of *Dar al-Imara* and was known as the *Cuarto del Caracol* (= Suite of the Spiral Stairs) in the Middle Ages, alluding to the four staircases of this kind at the angles. This complex consists of today's *Carlos V* Halls and the Garden-cum-*Patio* called *Doña María de Padilla* in commemoration of the famous lady who lived behind its walls.

In the middle of the 14C Alfonso XI, the victor in the battle of *El Salado* (1340), ordered a hall built next to the former Almohad *Patio* of *El Yeso* in the *Alcázar* of Seville. It is called *Sala de los Consejos* (= Hall of the Councils) or *de la Justicia* (= of Justice) and is of an architectural style combining Christian elements and others of Islamic design. It marks the beginning of civil Mudéjar architecture in Seville and consists of a cubic construction covered by a magnificent coffered ceiling with octagonal trough-shaped caissons. The walls have flat niches with plaster work reminiscent of Toledo models and elegant friezes at the top with alternating coats of arms of the Order of *La Banda* and of the kingdoms of Castile and León. Rich polychrome plaster work lines the walls of this hall, which has a door at either end, one leading to the *Patio del Yeso* and the other to that of *El León*. In the centre of the white marble paving is a beautiful fountain from where the water flows through a small channel to the pool in the nearby *Patio del Yeso*. In this hall –according to the chronicles– *Maestre Don Fadrique* found his death at the hands of Don Pedro (plate 9).

In 1248 Fernando III *el Santo* (= the Saint) conquered the city of Seville and the *Alcázar*. From then onward it became the residence of the kings of Castile who at first lived in the Almohad palaces. *San Fernando* spent long periods of time there and died within its walls on May 30th, 1252 (plate 7).

8. *Alfonso X el Sabio.* (= the Wise) Cantigas. (Detail). Monasterio de El Escorial. Madrid

9. Hall of Justice

The latter was, in fact, the monarch, known by the nickname of *el Justiciero* (= the Just) (plate 10), who built the Seville Palace that was the most important civil building in the Early Middle Ages and became an outstanding landmark in the development of Mudéjar art and architecture. It was begun in 1364 and finished in 1366. Christian and Muslim master builders from Toledo and Granada took part in the works as did many other master builders from Seville, who raised the first really rich and sumptuous building for a Castilian king to live in. As was the custom at that time, the residence, which will be treated in depth when it is described, only had a ground floor with a couple of storage rooms upstairs; these are the centre of the reception rooms belonging to the Upper Royal House (plate 11).

10. Praying figure of *Pedro I el Cruel*.
Archaeological Museum. Madrid

11. Façade of King Don Pedro's Palace

The architectural integrity of this 14C palace is still preserved today, but the building was subject to different alterations and refurbishing in the course of several centuries to enlarge and adapt it for the new executive requirements. Their traces are evident, especially those left by the important works that took place in the reign of the Catholic Monarchs (plate 12), who stayed there for long periods of time and who were there when their son, Prince *Don Juan*, was born behind those ancient walls.

The rooms of the Upper Palace were transformed, and the whole sector was enlarged with halls and areas to be used in the winter, while the summers were spent in the cooler lower rooms. These changes were only the beginning of a series of works executed by the monarchs of the House of Austria, through which the Mudéjar Palace was completed with a very similar upper storey, thus creating a lower summer and an upper winter house.

12. The Catholic Monarchs. Convent of the Augustinian nuns. Madrigal de las Altas Torres. Avila

The result of this refurbishing are the lateral galleries flanking the portal of Granada design, where the pomegranates in the plaster work alone date these passages to after 1492, the year in which the city on the Darro was conquered. The so-called *Cuarto alto de la Reina* (= Upper Suite of the Queen) is of the same period. It is not connected with that of the King and consists of an ante-chamber, a bedroom and a private oratory, commonly known as that of the Catholic Monarchs, as well as Prince Don Juan's bedroom. A beautiful vantage-point was raised on the side facing the garden. In the 16C, outside the palace area, but still within the confines of the *Alcázar*, the Catholic Monarchs founded *La Casa de la Contratación de las Indias*, the Chamber of Commerce, on the site where Al-Muhamid's palace used to stand and which is described in documents as the *Alcáçar vieio*. Despite all kinds of ups and downs, some parts of the building are still preserved and are known by the name of *Cuarto del Almirante* (= the Admiral's Suite).

14. Empress *Isabel* of Portugal. Titian. El Prado Museum

The reign of the Emperor (1517-1556) is one of the important moments in the history of the Alcázar, coinciding with the days of glory and splendour of the city itself: Seville, 'the capital of universal commerce', 'the port of and gateway to the Indies'.

This is where the Caesar Carlos married the lovely *Doña Isabel* of Portugal. On the occasion of the imperial wedding the Venetian ambassador Andrea Navaggiero, the nuncio of Pope Clement VII, Baldassare Castiglione, Juan Boscán and possibly Garcilaso de la Vega happened to meet with far-reaching consequences for Spanish literature since through them the italic metres found their way into Spanish *Ars poetica* (plates 13-14).

The enormous riches which came to Seville in those years increased the income of the *Alcázar* immensely. As a logical consequence it was possible to execute the important works planned at the time. The medieval fabric would forever be marked by the Renaissance cover of Italian origin. The most important alterations took place in the Upper Palace, which was completed by adding the King's rooms in the south. In addition, the former medieval storage rooms were interconnected with the constructions from the times of the Catholic Monarchs and the whole area was turned into comfortable living quarters for the winter months.

13. King of Castile and the House of Austria. Frieze in the Ambassadors' Room

Among all these the most outstanding are those executed in the upper passages of the *Patio de las Doncellas* (= of the Maidens). Their reconstruction was begun in 1540 and did not finish until 1572 in the reign of *Felipe II*. The design was prepared by the royal architect Luis de Vega and executed in Seville by the *Maestro Mayor*[1] Juan Fernández (1537-1572). The new passages were refurbished in the Italian style with semicircular arches on Ionic marble columns resting on pedestals and balustrades of the same material. All the marble parts were cut in Genoa by Antonio María Aprilla da Carona and Bernardino da Bissone. These galleries replaced other passages with flat arches on brick pillars of a smaller size than those of today and decorated with plaster work of the Mudéjar kind (plate 15).

On the outside the spandrels of the arches and the upper area of the wall as far as the eaves as well as the spandrels on the inside and even the arch rings of the new galleries are filled with Plateresque plaster work which also extended to an internal frieze as the finishing touch of the doors and windows. The busts of the lady and the knight, which symbolized the Emperor and the Empress, together with *putti* figures, plant volutes, grotesques and emblems of the imperial heraldry decorated these passages, for ever leaving behind a mark of the Italian-style Renaissance.

In the lower Palace slabs of marble were used to pave the galleries of the main *patio* and two splendid ceilings were built, that of the old chapel known today as the *Sala del Techo de Carlos V* (= Hall of Carlos V's Ceiling; 1541-1543) and that of the left-hand bedroom of *El Cuarto del Príncipe* (= the Prince's Suite; 1543).

Other alterations affected the access area of the Palace, ie the *Patio de Banderas*, as well as the fringes on its left and right which were very deteriorated at the time. The whole sector consisted of a series of rooms to be refurbished. Just for the record they are listed as follows: *Cuarto del Sol* (= Suite of the Sun), which was the residence of the *Alcaide*[2]; *Cuarto del Cidral* (Citron Grove), the residence of the deputy *Alcaide*; the Royal Kitchens next to the Gothic Palace (plate 16); *Cuarto del Maestre*[3]; *Cuarto de los Yesos* and *Sala de la Justicia* or *del Consejo*, all of them around the *Patio del Yeso*. In the same years, finally, some stables with their entrance portal were built (1539-1542). These occupied part of today's *Apeadero*[4] and extended as far as the wall and the *Callejón del Agua*. The *Patio de Banderas* was known as the "first" or "Reception *patio*" and it gave access to the main entrance of the *Alcázar* in the 16C. Surrounding it were the living quarters for the civil servants employed by the Palace.

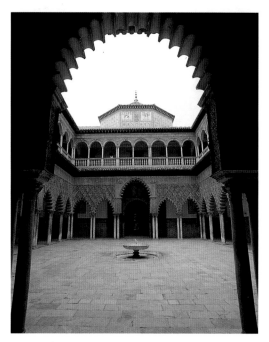

15. *Patio de las Doncellas*. Upper and lower passages. (General view)

The gardens were rearranged next by transforming the Muslim kitchen gardens into areas treated according to Renaissance tastes, without however losing the original Islamic structure.

Felipe II's reign (1556-1598) was another moment of glory for the *Alcázar* in the heart of the most universal place on earth. It was the period of greatest splendour for the Andalusian city, especially up to the decade of the seventies. Their intricate cosmopolitan nature was one of the outstanding features of the inhabitants. In 1580 the population was very large as it had doubled with regard to the first years of the century, while the riches in general, particularly silver and gold, continued to arrive in the harbour of Seville which turned into a real fair whenever the fleets from the Indies cast their anchors. All this brought enormous vitality to the Andalusian city, which was beautifully described by the numerous intellectuals and humanists who used to stay there and which was even compared with classical Athens and Imperial Rome. This flourishing prosperity produced the construction of *La Lonja* (= Customs House), which was the governing body of the commercial activity in Seville.

---

(1) Someone put in charge of Public Works by the Town Council

(2) Hist.: Governor of a fortress

(3) Hist.: Superior of any of the military orders

(4) Especially in Andalusian architecture: an entrance for carriages where the passenger(s) would alight by stepping on to a stone bench

16. Gothic Palace. (The exterior)

In those years the guest in the *Alcázar* was King Felipe himself who made his triumphant entrance in the spring of 1570 and was given a royal welcome by the people of Seville, described in great detail by the humanist Juan de Mal Lara. The monarch, who stayed at the Royal House for fifteen days, used its centre to inaugurate the new works that were about to be finished. It was during his long reign that the alterations which began in the times of the Emperor as well as other new ones to modernize the palace were concluded, but above all the ground plan was unified and given a very rational layout interconnecting the different existing parts.

The conclusion of the works in the *Patio de las Doncellas* undoubtedly incorporated one of the most important modifications. In 1572 the upper passages were finished and between 1560 and 1569 the ground floor was refurbished by replacing the old marble supports with Corinthian columns, carved by Francisco and Juan de Lugano as well as Francisco de Casona in their Genoese workshops.

At the same time the central arches of each gallery were stilted and tall pilasters were introduced and decorated with Plateresque plaster work which was also distributed over the walls of the arcade in combination with *tsebka* work and Mudéjar-style palms imitating Islamic ones. Later (1581-1584) the central area of the *patio* was paved with marble and decorated with a lovely fountain of the same material.

Apart from the alteration in the *Patio de las Doncellas*, a few other parts of the Upper Palace were repaired, among them the so-called *Cuarto de Hércules* (= Hercules's Suite) or *de las Cinco Cuadras* (= of the Five Stables), which is identified with the parts situated on the northern side, thus forming the façade of the palace facing the *Patio de la Montería*. Here some of the old medieval storage rooms were absorbed in the process.

Now another construction of a different nature must be given special attention. It is the *Corredor del Príncipe* (= Corridor of the Prince; 1589-1595) which was built to connect the Queen's with the King's rooms and to embellish the Palace façade facing the Prince's Garden. It has a magnificent ceiling the design of which is ascribed to Martín Infante. Behind the passage in the western part of the Upper Palace, other noteworthy parts were built, such as the Gala Dining room, as it is called today, and the beautiful ceiling of the Smoking (1591) and the Billiard (from around 1590) rooms, also ascribed to Martín Infante, apart from opening four balconies in the upper area of the *Salón de Embajadores* (= Ambassadors' Hall) and restoring its splendid dome (1599-1600). At the same time both ceilings of the ground floor rooms on the sides of the Ambassadors' Hall (1590-1598) were executed as well as that of *La Media Caña*, which is today's *Salón del Techo de Felipe II* (= Hall of Felipe II's Ceiling).

On the eastern flank there was the so-called *Cuarto de San Jorge* (= St George's Suite) which had an upper and lower storey and extended along the side facing the *Patio del Crucero* (= of the Crossing) or *de Doña María de Padilla*. There, important repairs were carried out to give it a pleasing appearance.

Another series of alterations worth describing are those in the Patio and the lower and upper storey of the *Cuarto de la Montería*, the latter being today's *Cuarto del Almirante*. First the wall separating *El Crucero* or *Patio de Doña María de Padilla* and the *Patio de la Montería* (1575-1576) was built. This wall finally linked the Royal Suite with the *Patio del Yeso*; after that the upper parts above today's Admiral's Suite were refurbished and made ready for use (1583-1590). Then the corridor before them, ascribed to the *Maestro Mayor* Antón Sánchez Hurtado (1584-1588), was built. Finally the staircase (1591-1593) connecting the *Patio de la Montería* with the Suite of the same name and with the Upper Palace was executed and thus became the main access to the building. As a result of these works, the *Patio* and *Cuarto de la Montería* were definitively linked with the palace itself, which was enlarged with the new rooms necessary to provide for the possibility of housing the Court.

Apart from these works other important repairs are made in the rooms around the *Patio del Yeso* and the *Cuarto del Sol, del Cidral* and *Cocinas*, situated around *El Crucero*. At last the former Gothic Palace was transformed into the Renaissance *Salas de las Fiestas* (= Halls for the Celebrations), which are known today as the *Salones de Carlos V* (1576-1588) and were called *Salas de las Bóvedas* (= Halls of the Vaults) in the 16C, referring to the vaults forming the ceiling. All these alterations mirror the important rebuilding activity which took place in the Palace during this period. At the same time the design of the gardens enters its second stage. They were enlarged and rearranged following the example of the Italian garden models.

After the death of the "Prudent" King, his son *Felipe*, the third of this name, occupied the throne of Spain. During the twenty-three years of his reign (1598-1621), Seville experienced a period of great prosperity, but also of decline; ie, a time of great contrasts. The first years of the century mirror a somewhat fictitious splendour still maintained by the fabulous riches that continue to be unloaded in the harbour of Seville. But in the course of the years they brought corruption and decline which reached unusual levels, above all in the middle of the century, ie, in the reign of his son *Felipe el Grande* (= the Great). The Palace of Seville, however, saw days of glory and sumptuousness. The building was further enriched by important new works that were undertaken in view of King Felipe III's announced visit, which never materialized, however, but from the preparation of which it benefited greatly.

Without a doubt, among the especially noteworthy alterations are the construction of the new *zaguán*[5] and *apeadero*[6] with a sumptuous, novel portal, all designed between 1607 and 1609 by the Milanese architect Vermondo Resta, who endowed the *Alcázar* with an entrance worthy of and appropriate to the status of the building; the conclusion of the works giving a new face to the *Patio de la Montería*[7] (1603-1609); and finally the construction of the "New Suite which continues with that of the Lord King *Don Pedro*" in the Upper Palace and its restoration, including the reception halls in the northern flank with the windows facing on to the *Patio de la Montería* (1592-1613).

Apart from these works new kitchens (1614-1615) were built in the area known as the *Cuarto del Asistente* (= the Assistant's Suite) as well as new stables (1615) in the *Callejón del Agua*. Both buildings were also designed by Vermondo Resta and raised to cover the requirements of the Court whenever it should come to Seville to stay. But the gardens underwent the greatest number of alterations and were turned into one of the most beautiful complexes among all those owned by the Crown of Spain. This period belongs to the third stage of their transformation.

Felipe IV's reign (1625-1666) was a crucial moment in the decline of Spain. Seville also mirrored the symptoms of decay of what used to be the most powerful nation on earth. The once numerous population was greatly reduced by the devastating effect of the terrible plague in 1649 while the fleets which carried the riches of the Indies found it increasingly difficult to negotiate the barely navigable Guadalquivir and many goods were lost before reaching their destination. All these circumstances together with those affecting the whole nation caused its decline. However, in the first years of Felipe IV's reign life was still relatively comfortable and for the *Alcázar* in particular this meant an important series of alterations made in view of the King's journey to and stay in the Andalusian city (1624) (plate 17).

This journey was organized by the powerful prime minister *Don Gaspar de Guzmán*, Count-Duke of *Olivares*, who was also the *alcaide* of the Seville *Alcázar* and who benefited greatly from the success of the King's sojourn in Andalusia. The main alterations in the *Alcázar* concentrated on the gardens and the building, which was totally refurbished to receive the royal guest for the three days of his stay. The Palace was again italianized in the Mannerist fashion of Vermondo Resta's works.

---

(5) Entrance hall of a building, usually designed for carriages.
(6) See explanation (4), page 10.
(7) *Montería*: A typically Spanish form of driving game.

17. *Felipe IV.* Velázquez. El Prado Museum

18. *Carlos II.* Juan Carreño de Miranda. El Prado Museum

After the King's stay in Seville, the Palace passes through a less brilliant period. Although some noteworthy alterations were made, the golden period of the building in the times of the Austrian dynasty had come to an end. The construction, however, of the grandiose *Corral de la Montería* in the *Patio* of the same name, called *del León* (1625-1626) today, deserves special mention. It was the largest theatre in Seville and had an oval ground plan, which was an important novelty. The entire framework was made of wood as was everything else in the building and a few years later this would be its ruin since the *Corral* was razed by a violent fire in 1691. However, it used to be the most comfortable theatre with the best acoustics in Seville. Next to the *Corral*, the so-called *Cárcel de la Montería* (= La Montería Prison) was built in addition to living quarters for the tenants of the theatre.

In the second section of the *Patio de la Montería* in front of the Palace façade the so-called *Herramenterías* (= tool sheds) were rebuilt and the Carpenters' Workshops were repaired. In the course of those years alterations were made to the living quarters of the civil servants in the *Alcázar*, grouped around the *Patio de Banderas*, and to the Stables and Coach Houses on its left-hand flank. In addition, other stables were built in the *Callejón del Agua* where the slaughter houses stood.

As regards the gardens, the arrangement of the last border was concluded, while maintenance and embellishing work took place in those parts

which were already finished. These alterations were the fourth stage in ordering the oldest garden section in the *Alcázar*. The Palace also had two kitchen gardens, *La Alcoba* and the so-called *Nueva* or *del Parque*. In the same period the Palace was also the scene of the famous literary circles organized around its *alcaide*, the Count-Duke of *Olivares*.

The Austrian dynasty comes to an end with the reign of *Carlos II,* Felipe IV's son and successor to the throne of Spain (1665-1700), a sickly young man, who tried to palliate his psychological disorders by attending exorcizing sessions which brought him the nickname of *el Hechizado* (= the Bewitched) (plate 18).

The decline of these years is a clearly visible fact. It was a period in which Spain was in great trouble: it was engaged in a war with other countries, the aristocracy was rebelling, it witnessed palace fights and intrigues, the economy had deteriorated tremendously and in addition there was no successor to the throne. The enormous national problems also affected the Andalusian city which lived through one of the least fortunate periods of its history. Seville Palace also reflects the absence of splendour at this time.

No new designs are executed and every effort is directed towards maintaining the building and gardens. The only outstanding event is the tragic fire on May 3rd, 1691, which burnt down the theatre –*Corral de la Montería*– and damaged the *Alcázar* itself as well as the *Casa de la Contratación*.

19. *Felipe V* and the Royal Family. Louis Van Loo.
(Detail). El Prado Museum

20. *Carlos III*. Mariano Salvador Maella. (Detail)

The House of Austria was succeeded by the House of Bourbon on the throne of Spain and upon Carlos II's death the Spanish Crown came to Philippe V of Anjou (1700-1746), the nephew of the Sun King. In the first stage of Bourbon rule, there were moments of great importance for the history of the *Alcázar* since the Royal Family together with the whole Court stayed there for five years. This memorable event was described in great detail by the Jesuit Antonio de Solís in his well-known *Olimpíada*. The city was at its finest to receive the royal guests who made their triumphant entrance on February 3rd, 1729. During this period the *Infanta María Antonia Fernanda* (November 4th, 1729) was born in the *Alcázar* of Seville. The news was celebrated with lights at the *Puerta de Jerez* (= Gate of Jerez) and an endless series of festive occasions in which the city took active part. It is also important to note that an international treaty, known as the *Treaty of Seville*, was signed in the *Alcázar* on October 20th, 1731.

Philippe V and Isabel de Farnesio must have enjoyed their stay in Seville tremendously always attending receptions, festive events and ostentatious public demonstrations, of which the inhabitants of this lovely Andalusian city are so fond (plate 19).

The Court left on May 16th, 1733. During the whole of that time, the monarchs had lived in the Palace of Seville in the company of their sons and future heirs, *Don Fernando VI* (1746-1759) and *Don Carlos III* (1760-1788) (plate 20). One of the best-known works of this period was the conversion of the upper Room above the *apeadero* into the Royal Armoury. During this long period the Lisbon earthquake took place (1755) and ruined a large part of the *Alcázar*. It marked the beginning of the most important 18C alterations and improvements which basically affected the *Patio* and the *Jardín de Crucero* where the square flower beds had to be filled to the level of their upper edges. In the Halls of the Vaults the so-called *Sala Grande* facing the *Patio* had to be rebuilt and was crowned with a lantern, while today's gallery was raised in front of it. At the opposite end a new façade was built with a beautiful portal in the centre, which gave access to a passage or gallery connecting the *apeadero* with the *Patio de la Montería*. After these works the *Alcázar* did not undergo any substantial changes.

21. *Carlos IV* and *María Luisa de Parma*. An etching

In the last third of the 18C the most distinguished Seville 'men of letters', among them especially Bruna, the Count of El Aguila, Jovellanos, etc, used to meet in the rooms called *del Asistente*, the assistant being *Don Pablo de Olavide*, who was the centre of the circle. The Palace of Seville was again visited in l796 by King *Carlos IV* accompanied by his wife Doña María Luisa de Parma and his children who spent eleven days behind its ancient walls (plates 21-22).

22. *Fernando VII* and *María Cristina de Borbón*. An etching

23. *Isabel II.* An etching

In the reign of *Isabel II* the Palace was used for some time by the Dukes of Montpensier who undertook important restoration works, which, to be sure, were not very orthodox. In this period the *Patio de las Muñecas* (= of the Dolls) was restored in the course of adding a mezzanine and a historicist gallery of little value. A pictorial restoration of most of the Palace took place at the same time.

The colours used for repainting were extraordinarily bright and of doubtful artistic and historical meaning (plate 23).

In the 20C the rebuilding activity of the Marquess of La Vega Inclán must be remembered since he transformed the former *Huerta del Parque* (= Kitchen Garden of the Park) or *del Retiro* into today's new gardens, which were finished by Gómez Millán. Also noteworthy is the period in which the post of curator of the building was held by the unforgettable *Don Joaquín Romero Murube*, who executed the works in the new parterre and in the *Patio de la Montería* with the help of the architect *Don Juan de Talavera y Heredia* (plates 24-25).

After that another architect, *Don Rafael Manzano Martos,* carried out an important number of restoration and maintenance works in the building while he was the curator, a post

24. *Alfonso XII*

25. *Alfonso XIII*

he held for a long time. First he gave a new form to the Prince's Garden, the *Patio del Asistente, de los Mareantes* and *de los Levíes* as well as to the buildings surrounding them. He also restored the Gala Dining-Suite, the upper passages or galleries of the *Prince's Patio* and Garden as well as the Oratory of the Catholic Monarchs. Outside the enclosure, in the area where the *Casa de la Contratación* stood in the 16C, he discovered and later described the domestic Palace of Al-Muwarak (11C) and its *Jardín de Crucero*. All these alterations took place in the sixties and seventies.

At a later stage (between 1983-1987) he discovered and restored the so-called *Mirador de los Reyes Católicos* (Vantage-point of the Catholic Monarchs), the upper galleries of the *Patio de las Doncellas* and another series of rooms in the Upper Palace; he also restored their roofs and the façade facing the gardens. In the upper and lower storeys of the Palace he replaced and repaired a large part of the flooring, that of marble as well as that of brick and small glazed tiles, apart from carrying out an endless series of maintenance work of the complex as a whole and of the garden. Finally, he also restored the old rooms of the *Cuarto del Maestre,* where the offices of the *Alcázar* are today, and adapted them to the new requirements; the *Patio del Yeso*, the Hall of Justice; the old Armoury above the *Apeadero* and

the *Apeadero* itself; the *Cuarto del Sol* or *del Alcaide*, and he further carried out the repair of the sewer in the *Patio de Banderas* where he found the remains of the palaeo-Christian Basilica of St Vincent Martyr as well as the renovation of House Number 2 in this *patio* together with the *Callejón* attached to it and the repair of some of the other houses surrounding it.

In the sector of the Gothic Palace his task included renovating the so-called *Sala Grande* or *de las Fiestas* and the restoration of the so-called *Pabellón de la China* at the end of the former *La Alcobilla Garden*, where from time to time the *Mediodía* group met, the most important member being *Don Joaquín Romero Murube.*

All these works have given life to this old building and have kept some areas in good order which had deteriorated and fallen into disrepair with the passage of time and because of the frail material used in their construction. At the same time the alterations made it possible to discover more about this beautiful complex, which, though of great age, has been perfectly adapted to the needs of modern life. The large number of the latest alterations described above were executed thanks to the initiative of the Board of the National Heritage Trust as well as the important support received from the Office of the Director General for the Heritage of Art and Culture Council of Seville.

III. AN ITINERARY
through the Palace and its Gardens

Puerta del León (plate 26)

Today the main entrance to the Palace of *Los Reales Alcázares* is *La Puerta del León* (= Lion's Gate). The name comes from the ceramic figure on top of the gate. It is a rampant heraldic lion with a cross and device between its claws, where the following inscription in Latin can be read: *Ad Utrunque.* The wall to which the gate belongs is part of the original 11C enclosure which was given the name of Al-Muwarak (The *Alcázar* of Benediction or the Blessed *Alcázar*).

The flank on the left-hand side of the gate which extends towards the *Santa Cruz* area encircled the first enclosure called *Dar al-Imara* (= the Governor's House) dating from the first years of the 10C.

26. *Puerta del León*

Patio del León (plate 27)

It is the first access *patio* which is a military esplanade in front of the palace, just as it was in Islamic times. Its boundaries are the curtain walls, and in the 17C (1625-1626) it was occupied by the huge *Corral de la Montería*, which was named after this and the following area. This sector has a series of gardens which were executed after the Civil War. At the back of the *Patio* there is a section of the wall with three large arches which give access to the *Patio de la Montería*. On its left-hand side there is the entrance gate to the Hall of Justice and on the right there was, in the 16C, the *Casa de la Contratación de las Indias*.

In the layout of an Arab palace, this patio would be the *Mexuar*, ie, the intermediate space between the street and the most private areas of the royal House. As was pointed out earlier, its old name was that of *Patio de la Montería*, perhaps because it was the place where the noblemen waited for the Kings to go hunting with them.

27. *Patio del León*

Patio de la Montería (plate 28)

It lies in front of the palace. Today its northern boundary is a section of the Muslim wall with the three arches giving access from the previous *Patio*. In other times it appears they had doors which were protected by guards to prevent uncontrolled access to the Palace. It is known that in the 17C (1608) the *zaguán* of the Royal *Patio* used to be in this area with a hall being built above it. On the right-hand side, before the Admiral's Suite, there is a passage or gallery the design of which is ascribed to Antón Sánchez Hurtado (1584-1588), a former *Maestro Mayor* of the *Alcázar*. This passage and the buildings behind it belonged to the so-called *Cuarto de la Montería*. The passage in question consists of two sections, each with semi-circular plain brick arches, resting on Ionic marble columns above and on Tuscan columns below. The ceilings of both galleries date from the 16C and are ascribed to Martín Infante. The upper gallery was glassed in in modern times. In the course of complementary works in the 18C after the Lisbon earthquake a series of buildings were raised on the left-hand flank and in front there is the superb façade of King *Don Pedro's* Palace.

There was a 17C project, kept alive until the following century, which consisted of surrounding the patio with galleries embracing the façade of the Palace. However only that of the right-hand flank was raised while the other two never passed the planning stage although their ditches were dug and the columns were bought.

28. *Patio de la Montería*. (General view)

Cuarto del Almirante and Casa de la Contratación (plates 29)

29. Passage and entrance to the Admiral's Suite

Behind the passage on the right flank of the *Patio de la Montería*, a door leads to the rooms known as *Cuarto del Almirante* (Admiral's Suite). In the 16C and 17C these rooms, which have an upper and lower storey, formed part of the *Cuarto de la Montería* and underwent important alterations. The door giving access to them is decorated with blue ceramics depicting castles and lions. Behind it there is a large rectangular hall with a 16C ceiling, known as the *Sala del Almirante* (= Admiral's Hall), where important historical memorabilia are kept of the relations between Spain and America. On this site, where Al-Muwarak Palace stood in the Early Middle Ages, the Catholic Monarchs founded the *Casa de la Contratacion de las Indias*, a fact which is remembered by a stone tablet with the following inscription: "In this *Cuarto del Almirante* Doña Isabel the Catholic Monarch founded the *Casa de la Contratación de las Indias* by a Royal Order dated January 14th, 1503, its first Governor being Sancho de Matienzo".

This was the place where the most important ventures of the discovery of the New World and Oceania were prepared and it brings to mind names such as Núñez de Balboa, Yáñez Pinzón, Juan de la Cosa, Enciso and so many others who, in the company of Christopher Columbus took the name of Spain to the farthest corners of the earth.

In the *Casa de la Contratación,* called the House of the Ocean by Pedro Mártir de Anglería, Hernando de Magallanes's expedition was also organized. After leaving the harbour of Seville, he began the first voyage around the world, which was successfully concluded by his companion Juan Sebastián Elcano who returned safely to the point of departure.

This place is therefore of great historical importance in relations of all kinds between Spain and America. The first section of this room is decorated with a series of paintings owned by the City Council of Seville and several portraits of personalities related to royalty, as for example the Duke of Montpensier and others (plates 30 - 31).

30. Duke of Montpensier

31. Duchess of Montpensier

32. *Isabel II*'s Bedroom

33. Romantic Museum

The last section of this room has been turned into a Romantic Museum by installing in it the bedroom furniture used by Queen Isabel II on her visits to Seville, as well as different objects of the period, such as beautiful fans, bronze sculptures, mirrors, etc... (plates 32-33). This room leads to the *Sala de Audiencia* (= Audience Hall) and Chapel of the *Casa de la Contratación*, which is a large square room covered by a rich 16C coffered ceiling with geometric patterns.

In its centre is a reredos with the *Virgin of Los Mareantes* by Alejo Fernández, the first representation connected with the Discovery and executed in Europe (plate 34).

34. Chapel with a reredos by Alejo Fernández

35. *Patio de los Levíes*

36. *Patio del Asistente*

The centre of the composition is the Virgin protecting a group of American natives with her open mantle. But in the foreground there is a series of figures among which Christopher Columbus is supposed to be the fair-haired gentleman in gilt clothes standing next to the Virgin and the Pinzón brothers from Palos de la Frontera (Huelva), very important mainstays of the glorious adventure as well as companions and friends of the Admiral, are thought to be those covered with a red cloak. On the left there is another series of personalities, probably governors of the *Casa de la Contratación* and the Emperor Carlos.

But special attention must be drawn to the bottom section with the different models of the ships available in Spain in the times of the Discovery. They are of scientific and historical interest and are depicted under the protection of the Mother of God. The walls of this chapel are adorned with coats of arms of the Spanish Admiralty from its foundation in 1248 and the first of its Admirals, Bonifaz, to the famous discoverer Christopher Columbus, who was received there upon his return from the second voyage by *Doña Isabel* the Catholic Monarch. Behind the windows of this room a number of small *patios* can be seen: the *Patio del Almirante, Patio de los Mareantes* and *Patio de los Levíes*, the latter being a reference to the beautiful, elegant loggia which was taken there from the Palace of the Levíes family. In modern times all these *patios* were organized in an area that used to be called *Corral de las Piedras* where the New Kitchens and offices of the *Alcázar* (1614-1615) were built in the 17C. In the 18C the whole sector was occupied by the living quarters of the city's Assistant. Today the name of *Patio del Asistente* is still preserved for the *patio* on which the living quarters used to centre and which has also been restored in recent times. At this point the name of Don Pablo de Olavide must be remembered: he and his literary circle met in the rooms of his home and were responsible for incorporating in the *Alcázar* the new trend of the Enlightenment which came from France (plates 35-36).

The Main Staircase (plates 37 - 38)

On the right, coming out of the *Cuarto del Almirante*, but without leaving the gallery, there is the large staircase giving access to the Upper Palace. It was built in Felipe II's reign between 1591 and 1593 together with other alterations that were executed in the *Cuarto de la Montería*, also called *Cuarto Nuevo* (= New Suite) because it had just been restored.

This is the main staircase of the building and has three sections leading to the upper floor of the passage or gallery by way of a double, semicircular arch resting on an Ionic marble column, in the same way as those of the upper gallery. It is covered by a richly decorated trough-shaped coffered ceiling on pendentives, adorned with polygonal caissons which have carved rosettes on the inside. The glazed tiles covering the walls are not the originals and come from the *Madre de Dios* Convent, but they are magnificent examples of 16C Seville ceramics. Also outstanding is the beautiful screen, ascribed to Francisco López who also made the banister of the staircase and the huge lantern of the ceiling.

Two pictorial masterpieces decorate the stairs on the way up: a large painting of the Virgin appearing to a worshipper by the Seville painter Francisco de Roelas and a historical-military subject by the hand of Federico de Madrazos showing the appearance of a soldier, a painting which obtained the gold medal in the Paris Exhibition of 1901.

Upper Palace (plate 39)

When you leave the staircase and enter the gallery on the left, there is a series of halls and rooms not open to the public. They were the upper *Cuarto de la Montería* in the 16C and 17C and have good coffered ceilings. In those centuries, especially in the 16C, they underwent important alterations to provide the extra rooms required to accommodate the Court.

38. Stairway leading to the Upper Palace. (Detail)

37. Stairway leading to the Upper Palace. (General view)

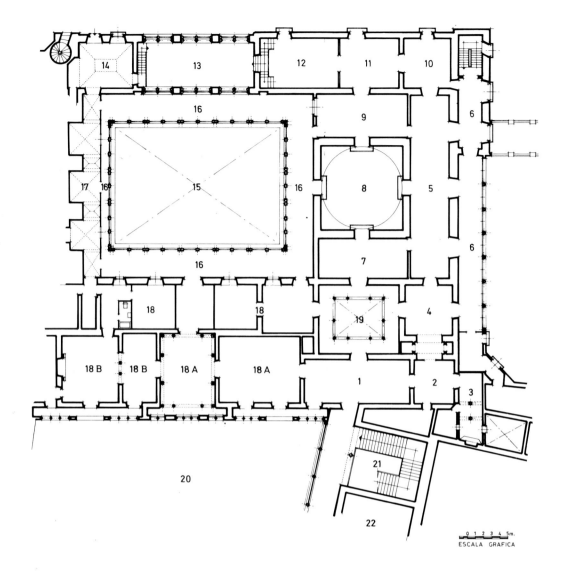

39. A storey of the Upper Palace

UPPER STOREY OF THE ROYAL SUITE

1. Ante-Chamber of the Queen. Today's Vestibule.
2. The Queen's Chamber. Today's Ante-Chapel.
3. Oratory. Today's Chapel of the Catholic Monarchs.
4. Prince Don Juan's Bedroom. Today's Ante-Gala Dining-room.
5. Gala Dining-room.
6. *Corredor del Príncipe.*
7. Upper Hall next to that of the Dome. Today's Billiard Room.
8. Hall of the Dome. Today's *Salón de Embajadores.*
9. Upper Hall next to that of the Dome. Today's Smoking Room.
10. The King's Retreat. Today's small Hall.
11. Suite of the King. Today's Family Ante-Dining-room.
12. Suite of the King. Today's Family Dining-room.
13. New Upper Hall. Mirador of the Catholic Monarchs.
14. Suite of the Lizards.
15. *Patio de las Doncellas.*
16. Upper Galleries of the *Patio de las Doncellas.*
17. Suite of St George.
18. Suite of Hercules or of the Five Stables (16C).
    A. Suite of the Lord-King Don Pedro (17C).
    B. Suite which continues that of the Lord-King Don Pedro (17C).
19. *Patio de las Muñecas.*
20. *Patio de la Montería.*
21. Royal Staircase.
22. Suite of *la Montería.*

40. Vestibule or small Room of the Queen

41. Bedroom or Chamber

Vestibule (plate 40)

If you return to the head of the stairs and turn from there to the right, you come to the door which leads to the Vestibule of the Palace. This was the former Chamber which, together with another series of rooms, formed the *Cuarto Alto de la Reina* (= of the Queen), a reference to *Doña Isabel* the Catholic Queen, since the rooms were built in her time. It was also called the *Saleta de la Reina* (= the Queen's small Hall).

It is a rectangular hall with a magnificent coffered ceiling full of interlacing decoration, dating from the times of the Catholic Monarchs because everywhere there are the heraldic motifs of the yoke and the arrows as well as the motto *Tanto Monta*, the symbols of these monarchs. The walls are decorated with a collection of tapestries with sketches by Teniers and a few by Wouwermans. This room has a door leading to the upper galleries of the *Patio de las Muñecas*, another giving access to the Ante-chamber and a third on the right leading to the *Alcoba de la Reina* (= the Queen's Bedroom).

La Alcoba (plate 41)

It is a square room covered with a magnificent eight-sided, trough-shaped coffered ceiling and its walls are tapestried. On the right there is an area closed off by a beautiful screen, from where the Chapel is reached. The room is adorned with two good carvings of the Seville school representing the Child Jesus.

Oratory of the Catholic Monarchs

(plate 42)

It was built in the times of these monarchs, which explains the name, and used to be the private Chapel of the Palace. The ground plan is rectangular and the ceiling consists of extremely depressed vaults where the keys are pointed. The ribs rest on consoles in the form of Gothic *culs de lampe* and although they rise vertically at first they later turn curvilinear and are adorned with holm-oak branches and pomegranates. The keys are decorated with very pretty Gothic rosettes containing the

42. Oratory of the Catholic Monarchs

initials F and Y. At the beginning there is an area which is like a vestibule for the chapel. In the centre it has a very beautiful marble column with a capital decorated with Mudéjar geometric prisms (= *mocárabe)*, which supports two segmental arches with flamboyant traceries. The same motif, ie, arches resting on a centre column, is repeated later and with these elements a Moorish conception of space is achieved in a Gothic guise.

This miniscule area centres on a ceramic reredos-cum-altar, executed, signed and dated by Niculoso Pisano in 1504. This is one of the key items in the *Alcázar* of Seville and one of the masterpieces of the Spanish Renaissance. It was made by using the technique of the flat polychrome glazed tile which was brought to

Spain at the beginning of the 16C by the ceramist mentioned above, who left behind other important examples in the city and who began a tradition which had excellent followers in Seville and the *Alcázar* itself.

The reredos pays homage to Queen Isabel, the central subject being the Virgin Mary visiting her cousin. It is ornamented with the yoke and arrows, the heraldic emblems of these Spanish monarchs, as well as with their coats of arms and initials. But most outstanding is the beauty of the grotesque decoration, through which the Renaissance air becomes noticeable in this beautiful work of art, in which the perfection of the drawing and the vivid colours and lines radiate unusual power and brilliance.

Ante-Dining-room (plate 43)

The rooms of the *Cuarto de la Reina* were rounded off by yet another room which was directly connected with the bedroom. This was the bedroom of Prince *Don Juan*, the Catholic Monarchs' first child who was born in this *Alcázar* and who 'died from being lovesick', according to his epitaph. Today this room is known as the Ante-Dining-room of the Gala Dining-room. It is a square hall with a 15C coffered ceiling, where the door in one of the walls leads to the upper galleries of the *Patio de las Muñecas*, the door of another to the Gala Dining-room and the door of a third wall to the gallery or *Corredor del Príncipe*. Two magnificent *bargueños*[8] are the only pieces of furniture in this room.

43. Ante-Dining-room

Corredor del Príncipe (plate 44)

It was built between 1589 and 1595, ie, at the end of Felipe II's reign. Its design is ascribed to Lorenzo de Oviedo, the *Maestro Mayor* of the time. This passage was built to connect the *Cuarto de la Reina* with that of the King, establishing the necessary link in the west wing of the Upper Palace. In addition it embellished the façade of the building facing the Prince's Garden and, by way of the lower gallery, provided an exit towards the rooms in this area of the Palace, which from that moment had access to the garden mentioned before.

It consists of two galleries with eight semi-circular arches resting on nine white marble columns, of the Doric order below and of the Ionic order above. There is a floor between the galleries with windows separated by plain pilasters. It was to be one of the first Mannerist constructions in the *Alcázar* of Seville. The magnificently carved ceilings are ascribed to Martín Infante, at the time *Maestro Mayor de Carpintería* (= Chief Carpenter). Both are dated: the upper ceiling was executed between 1592 and 1594 and the date is inscribed in the centre of a rosette, while the lower ceiling was made between 1592 and 1595 with the latter year inscribed in a device on the right-hand side.

44. Prince's Passage or Gallery

The original iron handrail with turned balusters in the upper gallery disappeared when its arches were filled in in the last century and were replaced by wrought-iron Isabelline balconies. Today's railing and metal work are the result of the restoration carried out in 1969.

---

(8) Spanish cabinets with carved decoration, originally from Bargas (Toledo).

45. Gala Dining-room

Gala Dining-room (plate 45)

This is a very long, rectangular hall which is connected with the Prince's gallery, mentioned earlier, on the right-hand side and with the *Salón de Fumar* (= smoking room), with an upper balcony of the Ambassadors' Room and with what used to be the Billiard Room, today turned into the Dining-room of the Assistants. At each end there is a door, one leading to the Ante-Dining-room and the other to what used to be the "King's Retreat" (plate 46).

Initially this room must have been built in Felipe II's reign, but in the last century it underwent radical transformation which makes it impossible to imagine what it may have looked like. Today it has an Isabelline ceiling with the light coming through three skylights.

The lights of the Royal Factory of La Granja adorning this dining-room are magnificent, especially that in the centre, as is the rich collection of tapestries depicting vases with flowers, garlands and columns in the style of Pompeii, which embellish the walls of this beautiful room. Also outstanding are the 18C chairs and the sumptuous carpet.

46. King's Retreat

47. Family Dining-room

From the balcony leading to it, there is a splendid view of that extraordinary room that is the Ambassadors' Room and from here it was possible to observe the dances and soirées that were organized in it in other times.

In the two halls connected with the Dining-room, which were executed or at least renovated in Felipe II's reign, especially outstanding is the ceiling of the so-called *Salón de Fumar* built in 1591.

This date is inscribed in a caisson at either end. It is also ascribed to Martín Infante, the Chief Carpenter. It is elongated with curved ends resting on semicircular trunks and decorated with octagonal caissons which form rhombuses and small squares at the joints.

Inside each caisson there are lovely carved floral clusters with egg-and-dart mouldings along the edges. The whole complex rests on a frieze of consoles. The ceiling was executed with mouldings of different lines which further emphasize its beauty.

Salas de Infantes

The southern flank of the Upper Palace has a series of rooms the balconies of which face the gardens. They are known today as the *Departamentos de Infantes* since they used to be the living quarters of the King's children in other times. They still preserve their old layout, but today the rooms are put to conventional use. Thus one of the room is known as the Family Dining-room which is used for this purpose because it is next to the Gala Dining-room.

In the 16C these rooms were the *Cuarto del Rey* and they were built or renovated in the reign of the Emperor. The room occupying the corner or south-west angle of the Palace was known as the 'King's Retreat', ie, it was a place of work or relaxation for the private use of the monarch. It has a corner *mirador*[9] discovered during the latest restorations. Behind it there is another square room connected with the next hall which is known today as the 'Family Dining-room' (plate 47), through which the so-called *Mirador de los Reyes Católicos* (= of the Catholic Monarchs) is reached.

---

(9) A kind of balcony.

48. *Mirador* of the Catholic Monarchs

49. King Don Pedro's Bedroom

All these halls are covered with exceptionally beautiful coffered ceilings decorated with the imperial emblems sustained by friezes of Plateresque plaster work which dates their execution. The next hall is know as the *Mirador de los Reyes Católicos* mentioned above (plate 48). It is rectangular, elongated and was built in the times of these monarchs (15C). The longer walls have six double horseshoe arches supported by central double columns, placed in line with the thickness of the wall, facing the gardens and the upper southern gallery of the *Patio de las Doncellas.* The masonry handrails are decorated with stucco in Mudéjar geometric prisms on the outside and false Gothic traceries as well as the heraldic emblems of the Catholic Monarchs on the inside. It is a ceiling from the times of these monarchs.

In the 16C –during the reign of the Emperor (1541-1543)– this hall underwent far-reaching alterations and was turned into one of the warmest rooms, to be used in winter. For this reason the arcades were filled in and a French fireplace was built in the southern wall. The old ceiling was preserved, but it was covered with a new, lower ceiling. This room was described in documents as the *Sala Alta Nueva* (= the New Upper Hall). In the restoration executed between 1976 and 1977 it was returned to its original state by reopening the large windows and restoring its original ceiling. In the course of these works a stairway was built connecting with the 'Family Dining-room' next to it.

All these rooms have a large number of paintings adorning the walls. Among them especially outstanding are those of *Doña Isabel* II and the Duchess of Montpensier, her sister; the *Infanta* María Luisa Fernanda by the 19C painter José María Esquivel; those of Isabel II's children, lovely pastel portraits by Bernardo López representing the Prince of Asturias, later Don Alfonso XII, and the *Infantas* Doña Isabel, Doña Paz and Doña Eulalia. There are also some oil paintings by Parceriza from the Cathedral of Barcelona and some very beautiful vases from the Italian school. Attention must also be drawn to the 19C furniture in general with magnificent chairs, consoles and mirrors as well as the collection of lamps and carpets.

King Don Pedro's Bedroom

(plate 49)

It occupies the south-west angle of the Upper Palace, bordering on Alfonso X's building, ie, the Gothic Palace. This is one of the few rooms still preserved in the Upper Palace from the times of Don Pedro, in other words the 14C. Its age and Mudéjar style are confirmed by Moorish plant motifs and epigraphic decorations on the walls as well as the splendid ceiling with interlacing Mudéjar patterns, all of which are polychrome and gilded. It is a small square room which used to have two bedrooms with arches leading to the central room. The room on the right was made smaller when the neighbouring *mirador* was built. It also has three doors by which it is communicated with the upper gallery of the *Patio de las Doncellas,* with the upper passage above the gardens and with the *mirador* mentioned above.

In the 16C (1542) this suite underwent alterations and was then described in documents as the *Cuarto de los Lagartos* (= Suite of the Lizards). The renovation consisted of painting the walls, ceilings, doors and windows. It must have been at this time when the lintel of the entrance door from the upper gallery of the *Patio de las Doncellas* was decorated with four skulls and new Plateresque plaster work was added, the remains of which are found next to the door giving access to the *mirador.* Its subjects are *candelieri*, floral carvings, heads of cherubim and a naked figure of Herculean proportions. The only furniture is a dressing table and a silver table belonging to *Doña Isabel* II, which consists of minute, detailed silver work of the 19C.

50. Royal Office

Royal Office (plate 50)

This is one of the reception rooms in the northern flank of the Palace. Its windows face the *Patio de la Montería* and it provides the link with the private rooms. In one of the walls there are triple horseshoe arches resting on marble columns with 16C capitals, which lead to one of the lateral bedrooms. Originally, this room together with the other formed the upper Royal Chamber, which is the main and most sumptuous part of the Upper Palace, from which they were separated by this section with intercolumniation.

Private rooms of the Prince and the *Infantas*

From the previous room the eastern gallery of the *Patio de las Doncellas* is reached and from there other parts of the Palace, which have been extensively refurbished by very recent restoration, with the idea of adapting these rooms to new requirements. In the whole area there is a series of rooms facing the *Patio del Crucero* or *de Doña María de Padilla*. These are today the private rooms of the Prince and the *Infantas*.

In the 16C the whole of this flank of the Upper Palace included the so-called *Cuarto de San Jorge* (= St George's Suite), which bordered on the Gothic Palace, while some of the windows opened on to today's Chapel.

The Queen's Music Room

By way of the northern flank of the upper gallery in the *Patio de las Doncellas* you come to a room which was once known as the Music Room of the Queen, meaning *Doña Isabel* II. The piano in one corner of the room is a romantic model of the times of Chopin and it is one of the first of its kind made by the famous piano makers Erhard in Paris in the middle of the 19C.

The paintings embellishing this room are extremely valuable, especially the portraits of Carlos III and two Neapolitan princesses by Antonio Rafael Mengs and those by Vicente López representing *Doña Isabel* II holding a map in her hand and her sister, the *Infanta* María Luisa Fernanda, practising solfeggio.

51. Audience Room

Audience Room or Upper Royal Chamber (plate 51)

This is the most sumptuous part of the Upper Palace. Together with King Don Pedro's Bedroom, it is one of the only two rooms of the upper storey that remain of the original layout of the 14C Mudéjar palace. It was reached by way of the staircase of *Las Damas*, which has several ramifications and gave access from the second vestibule of the Lower Palace, from the *Patio de la Montería* and from the *Patio del Crucero* or *de Doña María de Padilla*.

It consists of a central rectangular room separated by three arches from a narrow gallery next to the façade of the palace. These arches have their counterparts in three murals decorating the other walls of the room and resting on marble columns, the shafts of which are of different colours, alternately pink, white and black, with re-used caliphal and other Genoese capitals of the Renaissance, gilt-coloured and very beautiful, in the lateral

bedrooms. The latter capitals are of the same kind as those in the *Patio de las Doncellas*. This is why the room was also called *Cuadra de los Mármoles* (= Marble Hall), which belonged to the *Cuarto de Hércules* or *de las Cinco Cuadras*, which included all the halls of the northern flank of the Upper Palace. The inscriptions and decoration in polychrome plaster, which embellish these walls, and the skirting of very original rare glazed tiles as well as the magnificent ceiling with interlacing patterns are clearly reminiscent of its Moorish past.

Initially the central room had two lateral bedrooms separated by a section with intercolumniation and can be identified as today's Royal Office and the Ante-Chamber. The windows provide one of the most surprising views of the *Alcázar* because the walls of the Cathedral with its slender tower, *La Giralda*, can be seen across the *Patio* and gardens of *La Montería*.

52. Ante-Chamber

The Ante-Chamber (plate 52)

This room lies between the vestibule and the Royal Chamber and it is profusely adorned. Especially noteworthy are the French chairs, the Flemish tapestries, the different consoles and gilt-framed mirrors as well as the countless clocks, which is why this room is one of the richest and most solemn as required by protocol.

The tapestries here are the oldest ones existing in the *Alcázar* and they belong to the Flemish collection by Juan de Raes *el Joven* (= the Younger), depicting the Story of Cupid and Love. They are also signed by their author.

The series described above of the halls and rooms belonging to the Upper Palace façade were known in the 16C as the *Cuarto de Hércules* or *de las Cinco Cuadras*, a fact mentioned earlier. In the 17C it was known as the *Cuarto del Señor Rey Don Pedro*.

After leaving the Ante-Chamber, you are back in the vestibule. This is the point from where a visit of the Upper Palace begins. So far the most representative rooms have been analysed, but there is another series which, together with those already described, occupies the whole extension of this residential area. However, they are of no particular interest to a tourist visit. The main stairway leads back to the *Patio de la Montería* for a visit of the Mudéjar Palace (plate 53).

LOWER STOREY OF THE ROYAL SUITE

1. Vestibule.
2. *Patio de las Doncellas.*
3. Royal Hall.
4. Royal Bedroom.
5. Hall of the Wasted Steps.
6. *Patio de las Muñecas.*
7. *Cuarto del Príncipe.*
8. *Sala del Techo de los Reyes Católicos.*
9. *Corredor del Príncipe.*
10. Hall of the Barrel Vault. Today's *Salón del Techo de Felipe II.*
11. Hall of the Dome. Today's *Salón de Embajadores.*
12. Hall next to that of the Dome.
13. Hall next to that of the Dome.
14. Rooms of the Infantes.
15. Chapel. New Hall or Hall of the Coffers. Today's *Salón del Techo de Carlos V.*
16. *Patio de la Montería.*

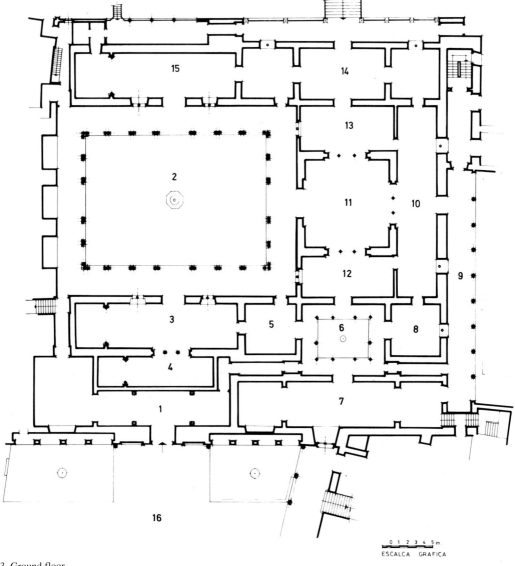

0 1 2 3 4 5 m.
ESCALCA GRAFICA

53. Ground floor

54. King Don Pedro's Palace. Portal

King Don Pedro's Palace (plate 54)

King Don Pedro I of Castile built this great palace considered one of the most important civil buildings in Seville, the construction of which was to have far-reaching consequences for Mudéjar art and architecture. Don Pedro is one of the controversial Spanish monarchs, his nicknames being the *Cruel* and the *Justiciero* (= the Cruel or the Just). But there is no doubt that he felt a special predilection for Seville, which he chose to be the capital of this kingdom and the scene of his numerous love affairs and infringements of the law.

Preserving the former old structures and with the help of carpenters and master builders from Granada, Toledo and Seville, he built this magnificent palace in a style and with material corresponding to Islamic taste. It is Mudéjar, a combination of Muslim elements and others of Christian origin, and it mirrors the enormous attraction which Islamic culture and architecture had for the Castilian monarchs. The works began in 1364, a date inscribed in the portal, and were finished in 1366, according to the doors in the Ambassadors' Hall.

The main façade rises at the back of the *Patio de la Montería* and was considered the most beautiful, sumptuous and pure paradigm of Mudéjar architecture. This magnificent front is framed by two brick pilasters on marble columns and it is topped by splendid polychrome pine-wood eaves, a fundamental feature among the Almohads of the Seville Mosque and the Granada Muslims of *La Alhambra*.

The first section consists of two blind arches of Almohad tradition, which are prolonged in the form of *tsebka* walls and rest on small marble columns flanking the entrance door with a voussoir lintel decorated with grape vines, a sign that Toledo artists were at work here. The bosses reveal the influence of Cordovan works and the ceramic decoration comes from Muslim traditions. Above the voussoirs of the door, where the geometric prisms in the hewn stone are intertwined with the heraldic emblems of the Castilian royalty, there is a coupled window with beautiful, small multilinear arches and at the top a load-bearing lintel, clearly of Granada influence. An inscription there in Kufic letters on white and blue ceramics contains the device of the Nasrids: *And no one is the victor but Allah.*

The Castilian traces become evident in the inscription framing the lintel where it says in monastic Gothic letters: *The very high and very noble and very powerful and conquering Don Pedro, by the Grace of God King of Castile and León, ordered these* Alcázares *built and these Palaces and these portals which were executed in the year of fourteen hundred and two.* This date is of the Muslim hegira, while the corresponding Christian date –mentioned before– was 1364. Also of the same date are the lower lateral brick arches resting on brick pillars, which were discovered a few years ago, but which had remained hidden in two plain walls for centuries. The entrance door also had a screen in front of it, which was put there in modern times. The upper galleries date from the times of the Catholic Monarchs and were built after the conquest of Granada, proof of which are the small plaster pomegranates framing the windows and the atmosphere in general which is very reminiscent of Granada.

55. Vestibule

56. Ceiling of the Vestibule

Vestibule (plates 55 - 56)

Behind the door there is a small Vestibule which along an elbowed axis leads to the two main sectors of the Palace, on the right to the domestic or private area and on the left to the official part. Both features are typical of the conception of Islamic architecture which requires an entrance built at an angle to prevent a direct view of the Palace interior. The four columns framing the first part of the Vestibule have Visigothic capitals, three of which may come from the former Basilica of *San Vicente Mártir*, while the fourth is cut in the style of the Caliphate. The Vestibule is divided into three parts by very round, semicircular arches, the spandrels and archivolts of which are full of Mudéjar plaster work as are the friezes. The whole area has coffered ceilings, of which the two lateral ceilings are probably the originals.

After passing through an area in semi-darkness and a door with steps, the last section of the Vestibule is reached. It is extraordinarily luminous and there attention is drawn to the bottom of a stairway on the left. It was called *Las Damas* in the 16C and by way of several connections it leads to the Upper Palace, the *Patio de la Montería* and the *Patio del Crucero*. Also noteworthy are two small Almohad vaults in this area proving that the 12C constructions came as far as this point.

57. *Patio de las Doncellas*

Patio de las Doncellas (plate 57)

From the Vestibule –after passing through a
door with wooden wings painted with interlacing
patterns, which are superb Mudéjar examples of
Toledo carpentry– the main *patio* of the Palace
called *Las Doncellas* is reached. This was the
centre of the official life of the Court.

Today the original layout has been
renovated and altered very much by the
refurbishing carried out in different periods in
history. Originally it consisted of plurifoil
pointed arches supported by marble columns
with wooden cymas. These supports were
double along the passage and single, but
thicker, at the angles. These arcades, noticeably
Cordovan in origin, are prolonged by traceried
tsebka walls of Granada influence.

The centre of each flank is marked by a
larger arch. It is not known whether the
original *patio* already had a second storey, but
there is absolutely no doubt about the existence
–as early as in the times of the Catholic
Monarchs– of upper passages or galleries with
flat arches on brick pillars, decorated with
Mudéjar plaster work.

58. Glazed-tile skirting. *Patio de las Doncellas*

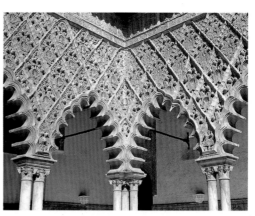

59. Plaster work. *Patio de las Doncellas*

This *patio* was built in the area between the Gothic Palace and today's Ambassadors' Hall, which had been the Throne Room of the Al-Muwarak Palace of the Banu Abbad, which underwent alterations in the course of these works. Therefore, between the buttresses of the wall bordering on the Gothic Palace Moorish divans were built so as to be able to enjoy the view of the lovely *patio.*

The central area may have had a garden in the form of a cross and four paths with streams flowing through them symbolizing the four rivers of the earthly Paradise. The flooring of the passages may have consisted of rough-face bricks and small glazed tiles. Beautiful glazed-tile skirtings with interlacing patterns inspired by those of Granada and dating from the 14C embellish the walls of the surrounding galleries. The appearance of the design is not a matter of chance, but deliberate, where each piece fits perfectly into those around it. Through good luck and despite repeated restoration, they have reached the present in good repair (plate 58).

The plaster work lining the arcades and facings on the inside of the passages is persistent proof of Cordovan and Granada traditions, as for example the inscription on the friezes with the well-known motto of the Nasrids: *Only Allah is victorious* (plate 59).

During the Renaissance this *patio* underwent important alterations which have been described in earlier pages. Basically the upper passages or galleries are rebuilt in the Italian style and decorated inside and outside by Plateresque plaster work, remains of which can still be found in the southern and western passages. The facing at the back of the eastern passage is full of plaster work and has nothing to do with the original building nor with the restoration done in the 16C. It is the result of very recent alterations.

By using moulds made from the remains of the Plateresque plaster work and a material different from the original, a recent attempt has been made at restoring these galleries to how they used to be in the 16C.

The lower passages, which were renovated at the same time as the upper galleries, also clearly show the mark of alterations in the imperial heraldic emblems scattered around the friezes and in the adorning plaster work in general, where Plateresque and Mudéjar motifs are mixed in the columns and in the marble flooring of the *patio* and its galleries which were to give a more classical air to the whole.

There is no question that the Renaissance combines perfectly with Mudéjar motifs and the *patio* in general does not lose its medieval image.

Bedroom of the Moorish Kings

(plate 60)

In the right-hand gallery of the *patio* there is the entrance to the hall commonly known as the *Dormitorio de los Reyes Moros* (= see heading) which may have been the Royal Suite. It consists of two parallel rooms with two bedrooms which are reached through an arch with a decoration of interlaced arches and another of the round trefoil kind. The exterior was the Royal Chamber and the interior room the monarch's summer bedroom, with a separation of a triple intercolumniation of Cordovan origin between them. This room is reached through a round, semi-circular arch with three lovely traceried plaster lattices deeply marked by Islamic incisions. It gives access to the northern gallery of the *patio* and has beautiful doors decorated with plant motifs carved by Toledo artists. Such doors are known as *gorroneras* and when they stay open and are folded back against the wall they also have a decorative function imitating beautiful tapestries with interlacing patterns. On either side there is a coupled window with a beautiful marble mullion and re-used caliphal capitals.

The ceiling of the first room is of great value. It combines interlacing geometric patterns with Renaissance motifs at the tapering ends of the wooden elements. Also oustanding is the plaster work of the friezes and of the frames of the arches, doors and windows.

60. Bedroom of the Moorish Kings

Patio de las Muñecas (plate 61)

From this area a small hall known as the *Cuadra de Pasos Perdidos* (= Hall of the Wasted Steps), which has a beautiful ceiling of the times of the Catholic Monarchs, leads to the *Patio de las Muñecas*. This is the area where the most private, domestic life of the palace took place. It is a very small, fragile *patio*, full of refinement and very much like those in Granada. It appears that the marble columns were brought from Cordova in the times of Mutamid. Their beautiful capitals are of the caliphal kind. The asymmetric balance of its shorter sides is well designed and of great beauty.

From the vestibule at the entrance this *patio* can be reached directly through a narrow elbow-shaped corridor, thus giving direct access from the residential area to the main *patio*, without having to cross the official area.

On the northern flank there is the entrance to the *Cuarto del Príncipe*, and from the southern gallery the Ambassadors' Hall and other rooms of the court sector are reached.

In the 16C and 17C it had an upper gallery with segmental arches on marble columns and railings of the same material. But in the 19C the architect Don Rafael Contreras added a floor between both galleries as well as a historicist gallery and a glass roof, which gave it its present look. The plaster work also underwent great changes in the course of these alterations although there are remains of the original work in the spandrels of the larger arches, in the *tsebka* walls of the smaller arches, the friezes of the interior walls and the rectangular decoration around the doors in the different walls. The upper part is embellished by the use of a large number of mouldings from *La Alhambra*.

61. *Patio de las Muñecas*

62. Prince's Suite. Ceiling by Juan de Simancas

Cuarto del Príncipe (plate 62)

The main entrance is that of the *patio* described above by using the northern gallery. It has a central hall with bedrooms at the ends, similar to those found in *La Alhambra*, and originally it was probably the Queen's summer room. It is called the *Cuarto del Príncipe* (= Prince's Suite) with reference to Don Juan, the son of the Catholic Monarchs, who was in fact born in this *Alcázar* in the summer of 1478.

The ceilings of these rooms are very beautiful, that on the right being an elegant trough-shaped, but much renovated, coffered ceiling and that on the left being a magnificent example of a flat ceiling with square caissons separated by curved lintels imitating Plateresque balusters. Each of the caissons is decorated inside with interlacing patterns and cones and the whole ceiling is richly painted and gilded. The frieze in the Plateresque style has a device with the following inscription: *This work was completed in 1543. It was carried out by Juan de Simancas. It was gilded and painted in 1854.*

The front wall of this bedroom has a screen which gives access to the Prince's Garden and next to it there is a staircase which leads to the Oratory of the Catholic Monarchs in the Upper Palace. The floorings of these rooms are of recent date.

Sala del Techo de Isabel la Católica or de los Reyes Católicos

When you leave the *Cuarto del Príncipe* and pass through the small arch that leads to the narrow passage giving access to the Prince's Garden, you will find an arch connecting the *Patio de las Muñecas* with this square hall, which has a most beautiful ceiling with inlaid interlacing patterns, dating from the times of the Catholic Monarchs. There is a frieze decorated with the yoke and arrows and the heraldic emblems of the Catholic Monarchs, all of which alternate with squares painted in the Plateresque style. It has a coupled window facing the Prince's Garden and a door giving access to the hall called *Techo de Felipe II* (= Felipe II's Ceiling). The plaster work adorning the inside frame of the entrance ceiling and that of the door to the next room are identical, but not so the corresponding coupled window. Attention should also be given to the period brick flooring with small glazed tiles.

63. Hall with the Ceiling of Felipe II. (General view)

Salón del Techo de Felipe II

(plate 63)

The previous room leads to this room the name of which comes from the fact that the ceiling was built in the times of that monarch, ie, between 1589 and 1591. In documents it is also called *Sala de la Media Caña* (= Hall of the Barrel Vault) making reference to the form of the ceiling. It is a rectangular room and the longest of those in Don Pedro's Palace. In the centre of the southern wall there is an arch with Mudéjar plaster work, which has a grille communicating with the Prince's Garden. It is flanked by two coupled windows and has modern doors and plaster work. In the 16C, ie in the years mentioned above, a door was opened in the wall to communicate the room with the lower gallery of the *Corredor del Príncipe*.

In the opposite flank there is a large, very depressed ogee arch framing a triple horseshoe arcade on beautiful marble columns with caliphal capitals, giving access to the Ambassadors' Hall. This is the so-called *Los Pavones* Arch referring to the decoration of the spandrels. Also especially outstanding is the beautiful frieze above the triple arcade, which consists of winding carvings forming circles, in the centre of which there are alternating gilded silhouettes of eagles and other birds, some of them pecking at the heads of other smaller birds. Three traceried lattices occupy the upper part. This is a magnificent set of Mudéjar plaster work the subject of which is inspired by Persian weaving patterns.

The remaining plaster work of the interior friezes and the rectangular frames around the doors was heavily repainted in the restoration carried out in the 19C. Before that they were touched up in the 16C. In the same wall, flanking the above *Los Pavones* Arch, there are two doors leading to the lateral bedrooms of the Ambassadors' Hall. And in the flank at the back there is a third door which gives access to the hall next to the Dining-room mentioned earlier.

Looking at the lovely ceiling of this large room, it should be remembered that its design is ascribed to Martín Infante, at the time *Maestro Mayor de carpintería*. It consists of square caissons with a varied pattern of geometric carvings inside in alternating order along the surface. The whole ceiling was originally painted and gilded by the painter Baltasar de Bracamonte.

64. *Los Pavones* Arch

Salón de Embajadores (plate 64 - 65)

Los Pavones Arch leads to the main hall of the palace. This square, domed room was the former *cubba* belonging to the Al-Muwarak Palace of the Banu Abbad. It was in fact their Throne Room and was called *Al-Turayya* (= Hall of the Pleiades).

65. Ambassadors' Hall. (General view)

In that period –11C– there was only this construction which was facing west, ie, the opposite way it faces today. It may have had a portico consisting of three parts and its main entrance would be today's *Los Pavones* Arch. It was flanked by two bedrooms separated from the central area by triple horseshoe arches on pink marble columns and caliphal capitals, which reproduce those preserved in the *Salón Rico* (= Rich Room) in Medinat al-Zahara and the outlines of which have survived.

66. Dome in the Ambassadors' Hall

67. Balcony in the Ambassadors' Hall

It had a beautiful wooden dome studded with stars symbolizing the Universe, but it was simpler than today's. It is also a fact that all the elements of this room were a direct copy of the *cubba* of the same palace, ie Medinat al-Zahara (plate 66). All the stuccoed and painted walls were covered with verses by the Sicilian Ibn Handis (plate 67).

In the 14C this room was renovated and a door was made leading to the *patio* that had just been built, ie the *Patio de las Doncellas*. Thus its orientation was also changed, but not the use it was put to: the Throne Room for the Castilian monarchs. In that period the walls were covered with magnificent glazed tiles depicting interlacing patterns (plate 68). Despite the restoration undergone over the centuries they have reached the present in good repair.

Also of the same period are the magnificent doors, which consist of two carved pine-wood wings with gilded and polychrome plant motifs and the corresponding wickets. It is a rich work of interlacing patterns with inscriptions in Arabic praising Allah and the sultan, and others in Latin taken from the Scriptures. There is the date when this magnificent work was executed, ie 1366, and who participated in it: master builders from Toledo.

Also outstanding is the rich plaster ornamentation with geometric designs, plant motifs, shells, heraldic symbols and inscriptions which cover the walls as if they were magnificent tapestries. Finally, there is the wooden dome or Half Orange, which has been the name of the room since time immemorial and in documents it was called *Cuadra de la Media Naranja* (= Hall of the Half Orange).

Today's ceiling replaced that of the Banu Abbad and according to an inscription preserved in the ceiling, was carved in the times of King Don Juan II of Castile, in 1427 to be precise, by the *Maestro Mayor de carpintería* Don Diego Ruiz.

68. Glazed-tile skirting in the Ambassadors' Hall

69. Ceiling in the lateral bedroom

This magnificent dome comes as a breathtaking surprise to the visitor because of its proportions and above all the beautiful traceried interlacing patterns, richly gilded and polychrome. It appears that the small mirrors were placed there by 19C restorers. It is considered a real masterpiece of its kind among those preserved in Spain. It rests on a frieze with alternating castles and lions, supported in turn by a gilded crown with geometric patterns forming an eight-point star. The circular plan gradually turns into a square through the pendentives consisting of richly adorned gilded geometric prisms (= *mocárabe*) at the corners. Underneath there is a wide border of ornamental Kufic inscriptions on a blue background, where the most eye-catching parts are those decorated with thirty-two female busts by Diego de Esquivel in 1598. After that there is another border with castles and lions and a broad frieze with shrine-like Gothic niches framing the portraits of the Spanish kings from Reccesvinth to Felipe III. They were executed between 1599 and 1600 and are also ascribed to Diego de Esquivel.

On every side the series of portraits is interrupted by a wrought-iron balcony made by the craftsman Francisco López between 1592 and 1597. It is the most important wrought-iron work executed in the *Alcázar* in the Modern Age. This hall is known as that of *Embajadores* (= Ambassadors) because this is what it says in the Arabic inscriptions decorating the door and it comes as a very pleasant surprise to those who see it for the first time because of its balanced proportions and enormous wealth, which turn it into one of the most valuable rooms in the *Real Alcázar* and in Mudéjar architecture as a whole.

The lateral bedrooms were restored at different times. Thus Gothic artists have left their mark in the plaster work depicting vine, oak, fig and holm-oak leaves, as well as flat silhouettes of people and animals. The ceilings were executed in Felipe II's reign between 1590 and 1598 and are also ascribed to the *Maestro Mayor de carpintería* Martín Infante (plate 69). One of these rooms faces the *Patio de las Muñecas* and the one opposite faces a room known as the *Comedor* (= Dining-room).

Dining-room

It is a room between two others on the southern flank. All of them together must originally have been the rooms or bedrooms of the *Infantes* and are symmetrical to those behind the Ambassadors' Hall in the northern front. They were extensively renovated in the 19C. The windows and doors face the Garden of *Las Galetas* (= the Galleys) by way of a passage or gallery. The central room still has a white marble plaque in memory of the fact that Her Highness Doña María Isabel de Orléans y Borbón was born there on September 21st, 1848. The next room, which has a small door leading to the *Patio de las Doncellas*, is the ante-room of the hall called *Techo de Carlos V* (= Carlos V's Ceiling). The flooring of these rooms was recently renovated.

70. Hall with the ceiling of *Carlos V.* (General view)

71. Ceiling of *Carlos V*

Salón del Techo de Carlos V

It lies in the southern flank and must originally have been the palace chapel, the hall of which used to be the nave and its bedroom the presbytery before it was transformed for domestic use. The religious purpose of these rooms is proved by the border of inscriptions framing the door of the passage, where a well-known Eucharistic prayer is reproduced (plate 70).

During the Emperor's reign the old Mudéjar ceiling was replaced by that of today, which is one of the best Renaissance examples treasured in the *Alcázar*. It was executed between 1541 and 1542 and its design is ascribed to Sebastián de Segovia, at the time *Maestro Mayor de carpintería*, who planned a ceiling consisting of octagonal caissons with rhomboid patterns at the joints bordering on richly carved mouldings (plate 71).

In the centre area there are thirteen caissons with carved, almost fully visible busts representing warriors, ladies, young and old men, the first two of which being a clear reference to the Emperor Carlos and the Empress. The remaining caissons are adorned with lifelike bunches of flowers. The ceiling rests on a beautiful, very Plateresque frieze executed by Melchor de Morales. In the 16C this room was known as the *Sala Nueva Baja* or *Sala de los Artesones* (= Room of the Caissons), making reference to those in the ceiling.

Patio del Crucero or de Doña María de Padilla

After leaving again by the main door leading to the *Patio de la Montería* and turning right there is an 18C gallery connecting the *apeadero* with the *patio* mentioned before. In the centre of this gallery and on the right-hand flank, there is the entrance door commonly known as that of *Doña María de Padilla*.

The whole sector was extensively renovated in the course of the 18C works after the Lisbon earthquake of 1755.

On the left-hand flank, occupying the former rooms of the so-called *Cuarto del Maestre* and *Del Yeso,* there are today's offices of the *Alcázar.*

In the middle of the 13C Alfonso X *el Sabio* (= the Wise) rebuilt the Almohad palace again, turning it into a Gothic palace and restructuring the cross-shaped garden. This part, which included today's *Patio de Doña María de Padilla* and the halls called *Carlos V,* were known in the Middle Ages as the *Cuarto del Caracol* (= Suite of the Spiral Stairs), which is popularly thought to have been the area of Doña María de Padilla's private rooms. This woman had great influence during Don Pedro I's reign.

The *patio* had suffered during the Lisbon earthquake in the 18C and had to be reinforced by being filled in up to the level of the upper borders, which is the way it looks today with the four squares of myrtle.

At the northern front a connecting gallery was built with a Baroque door, and on the southern flank the passage or gallery before the Gothic halls of the Ionic order, all of which was executed by the engineer Sebastian van der Borcht. The garden below ground level has been recently restored and the material blocking the arches eliminated.

72. Gallery before *Carlos V's* Halls

Salones de Carlos V

The Halls of Carlos V as they are known today are the site of the Gothic Palace mentioned above which was rebuilt in the times of Alfonso X *el Sabio* in the middle of the 13C. It is therefore older than the Mudéjar Palace (plate 72). It consisted of four rooms, two of them parallel to the *patio* and today's gardens, and the others, one of them being today's chapel (plate 73), lie perpendicular to the end of the two mentioned previously. They had rib vaults resting on pillars and outside there was a terrace designed as a parade ground.

73. Chapel

The exterior has solid buttresses forming crenellated towers, while the four angles have four larger towers with spiral staircases inside, justifying the name *Cuarto del Caracol* which it was given in the Middle Ages.

In the 16C they were called *Salas de las Bóvedas* (= Halls of the Vaults) or *de las Fiestas* (= of Celebrations) probably because they may have been used for the banquets held on the occasion of imperial weddings. In that period they underwent great alterations by the removal of much of their medieval austerity and the addition of elements emphasizing the modern Renaissance trend of these alterations. Thus the walls were lined with high skirtings of beautiful glazed tiles executed by Cristóbal de Augusta between 1577 and 1583, where homage is paid to the Emperor and Empress. The pillars are replaced by Mannerist consoles designed by Asensio de Maeda (1577-1578), the vaults of the two centre halls are painted and lovely grilles are made for the windows which at the same time were enlarged to provide more light (plate 74).

74. *Sala Grande*

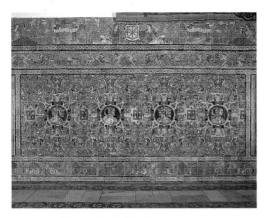

75. Glazed tiles by Cristóbal de Augusta

76. Hall of the Gardens

After the earthquake of 1755, the Palace was greatly weakened so the first hall had to be redesigned and rebuilt. It was known as the *Sala Grande* and faces the *patio* (plates 75-76). In the last few years it has been restored extensively with new plaster work in the vaults, new door frames, flooring and marble skirtings. In this room the enormous and beautiful tapestries of the Conquest of Tunis by Carlos V can be admired. They were painted by Juan de Vermayen and woven by Guillermo Pannemaker (1535-1554).

Garden of El Alcázar

The itinerary through the gardens depends a little on the visitor's choice. But there is a way of seeing the gardens that may be considered ideal and this is the one recommended in the following. The first to be visited are those next to the walls of the palace, after that those forming the second section which lies parallel to the first and then the third. These are the oldest gardens of the Palace. After passing through *La Puerta del Privilegio* (= Door of the Privilege) in the wall, the so-called New Gardens are reached. When this part of the visit is finished, there is *La Puerta de la Marchena* which leads to the *Apeadero*. On the way there is another series of gardens which lie between the wall and the buildings of the Palace. A brief description of this beautiful area follows below. The first sector was originally occupied by the Muslim

77. Garden of *El Estanque*. (General view)

orchard and corrals and by the so-called *Huerta de la Alcoba* inside the walls of the Palace. On the site where the Islamic gardens lay and without their original structure being eliminated, the oldest gardens of the *Alcázar* in Seville were designed in the course of the 16C and 17C. Each fragment received a specific treatment following the Italian models and they are a real stage where myth and legend play an important role. These gardens were the model and source of inspiration of the Renaissance garden in Seville. The so-called *Jardines Nuevos* (= New Gardens) are beyond the wall, where the exterior orchards of the *Alcázar* used to lie in other times, and were designed in the 20C.

79. Gallery of *El Grutesco*

Garden of El Estanque

Coming from the Halls of Carlos V, the first garden is the so-called Garden of *El Estanque* which receives its name from the large pool-like reservoir in its centre (plate 77). Since time immemorial it was used to irrigate the Muslim orchards. On its northern side there is the main entrance to the gardens and a low bower of two semi-circular arches on a central marble column. Above it there is a path ending at the curtain wall on the right-hand side and leading to the *loggia* or *mirador* on the left. The latter consists of triple arches on double marble columns and iron handrails. It communicates with the area bordering on the Gothic Palace. This whole front was renovated between 1573 and 1575. The upper *mirador* dates from 1612 and was built by Vermondo Resta. In the centre of the pool there is a lovely bronze fountain representing the god Mercury (plate 78) on an elegant pedestal decorated in a life-like fashion by the sculptor Diego de Pesquera and cast by Bartolomé de Morel. Both artists are also the authors of the decoration on top of the balustrade which consists of four lions with their coat of arms occupying the corners and eighteen balls with pyramidal tops. Originally all of them were gilded and some remains of the gold can still be seen. The date of these alterations lies between 1567 and 1577. The eastern flank was a place where the former Almohad fence used to be. Between 1612 and 1621 it was beautifully hidden by the Gallery of *El Grutesco* (plate 79), a magnificent construction by the Milanese architect Vermondo Resta. It begins at this point and continues as far as the back of the gardens. Initially it was decorated with beautiful paintings by Diego de Esquivel, representing the River Guadalquivir with boats and ships and vine leaves with grapes on top, as a symbol of Seville prosperity at that period. Today's paintings are a clumsy copy of the originals. In the remaining gallery there were paintings of heathen gods and goddesses. The southern flank of this garden has masonry benches lined with glazed tiles, leaning against the handrail by which it is separated from the Garden of *Las Damas*. From this area an upper path leads towards the Prince's Garden and provides a view of the gardens as a whole. On the western flank there are the steps leading from this area to the former Garden of *La Danza* or *Las Danzas*. This flight of steps dates from the 18C and replaced others built in 1610.

78. A statue of Mercury

80. Garden of *Las Danzas*

82. Garden of the Labyrinth or of Troy

Garden of La Danza or Las Danzas

It is a rectangular area divided into three sections (plate 80). The first at the top has two marble columns which in the 16C and 17C had a satyr and a dancing Maenad on top, which together with the other figures in the trimmed myrtle hedges gave their name to the garden. There are some steps giving access to the second section which centres on a small, beautiful glazed-tile fountain with a 16C spout surrounded by masonry benches lined with glazed tiles. On the right there is an arch with a grille, which leads to the garden below ground level known as the Garden of *El Crucero* and on the left there is a door giving access to the Garden of *Las Damas*. This central path paved with brick has two lines of *burladores*, ie, small holes spouting water, the play of which enlivens and embellishes this part while at the same time the continuous bubbling sound is music to the ear.

Perpendicular to it there is another path leading to the next garden area by way of an arch closed by a grille. On the left-hand side there is a small, hidden window which provides a view of the Garden of *Las Danzas*, while the two masonry benches on either side of the arch are an invitation to rest.

Gardens next to the Palace

In the 16C and 17C the garden bordering on that of *Las Danzas* was known as the Garden of the Labyrinth or of Troy, probably because of the designs of its paths. It has a beautiful modern fountain and is flanked by two passages or galleries, especially outstanding of which is that on the left because of the beauty of its elements and the use of roughly hewn ashlars. It is ascribed to Vermondo Resta and was probably executed in 1606 (plate 81).

The area towards the back was called Garden of the Galley, which is a reference to the myrtle hedges trimmed in the shape of ships for decoration. It also has a passage probably dating from the 16C and although it is covered by a pergola the carved pedestals date from that period (plate 82). A wall with a central arch is the boundary of this garden, separating it from the next called Garden of the Flowers in the 16C (plate 83). It consists of a pool which borders on the wall described and which is lined with beautiful glazed tiles of the

81. Passage of the Garden of Troy

83. Garden of the Flowers. Portal of the niche

84. Prince's Garden

pisano kind, which are made following the technique of the flat, polychrome glazed tile brought to Seville by Niculoso Pisano, after whom it is named. In the back wall remains can still be found of grotesque decoration and terracotta figures.

Between 1589 and 1601 a grotto-cum-fountain was built on the western flank of the garden. It was adorned with numerous figures and shells, mother-of-pearl, snails and fish mouths and painted in bright colours. Later a very Mannerist niche was built and in its interior remains of the original grotto are preserved. Today it frames a bust of the Emperor. The garden centres on a small fountain of the Islamic kind.

The last garden of this first section is the Prince's Garden, named after Prince Don Juan, the first-born of the Catholic Monarchs. On the western side there is a passage also called the Prince's and described in previous pages, while in the south there is a second gallery

executed around 1976, which separates this garden from the old Garden of the Flowers. Both areas were originally connected by a flight of stairs. Its northern wall has a door giving access to the *Patio del Asistente*. The intersecting paths form four squares with vegetation, while the centre is occupied by a small modern fountain. In the 16C this garden also had a pool (plate 84).

The lush vegetation in all the gardens described consists basically of orange trees concealing the walls, many of which are very old.

On the other hand, there are very tall plants sown in modern times, which destroy the original symmetry. In the 16C and 17C there were a lot of figures treated in accordance with the laws of *ars topiaria*, ie, with bodies of trimmed myrtle and with painted heads or hands made of wood or baked clay. It is known that they included giants, satyrs, nymphs, ships, etc, but none have been preserved.

Garden of Las Damas (plate 85)

This is the largest of the oldest garden section in the *Alcázar*. It already existed as such in the 16C, but it was smaller, ie exactly half the size it is today. At the beginning of the 17C (1606) it was enlarged to form an enormous rectangle divided into eight squares bordering on the two main paths and the intersecting paths crossing the other two. At that time the brick wall was built with a set of doors and windows designed very much in the style of Vignola, although those built on the western flank were built between 1623 and 1624 on the occasion of King Felipe II's visit. The wall on the southern side was built in the 18C. (Plate 86).

85. Garden of *Las Damas*. (General view)

86. Entrance to the Garden of Las Damas

87. Large grotto

Also in the first years of the 17C the garden was adorned with a marble fountain at the crossing of the two main paths, with the statue of Neptune on top as well as a series of grottos resting on the wall where terracotta and lead figures represented different mythological fables.

In addition, the main and largest of all the grottos functioned as a hydraulic mechanism giving off programmed sounds thanks to the pressure of the water. In all the others there were birds, trumpets and an endless collection of musical instruments producing extraordinarily pleasant sounds (plate 87) . In the twenties the flooring was laid, two small, low fountains were built in the Islamic style alongside the main fountain and numerous *burladeros* were built along the garden paths, describing beautiful arches of water when activated.

It is impossible to leave out the Gallery of *El Grutesco*, the boundary on the eastern flank, which is a section that was executed between 1613 and 1621, with lovely vantage-points from where there are magnificent views of the gardens of the *Alcázar* as a whole.

The vegetation was also looked after carefully. The myrtle hedges were used as the boundaries of the gardened squares and the plants that grew inside, without reaching a great height, were trimmed to form heraldic emblems of the Spanish Royal House. This garden also had giants in the trimmed myrtle hedges with painted wooden heads and hands, standing guard at the entrance, the main gate. These giants were known to be Hercules and Antaeus fighting with each other. In view of all these elements in addition to the frescoes decorating the wall, its doors and windows, the grottos and the Gallery of *El Grutesco*, this garden looked quite different from what it looks today, with its taste for luxury, the importance of the sense of playfulness, the ambiguity of its elements, derived from Italian Mannerism. Due to the passage of time and the hands of men it has acquired a rustic, rural image, far removed from the idea governing its initial construction.

This garden, which was turned into the most beautiful and impressive of those belonging to the *Alcázar*, was one of the most important achievements of the architect Vermondo Resta and its influence was to be decisive for the Renaissance gardens in Seville.

Garden of the Labyrinth

Through a beautiful door situated on the right-hand flank of the Garden of *Las Damas* and after descending some steps, there is a garden built in the 17C and called the Labyrinth, as a reference to the way the vegetation had been trimmed (plate 88).

The centre is taken up by a polygonal pool with a grotto-like elevation which originally was Mount Parnassus and was adorned with numerous terracotta figures representing Apollo surrounded by the nine muses. At the top was the horse Pegasus. The only parts preserved today are the remains of animal heads found scattered on the elevation and what was left of the interior network of tubes from which the water spouted as if it really came from the entrails of the earth.

The labyrinth embracing this pool has disappeared completely as have the robots representing huntsmen, lions, red deer, etc. which used to be everywhere. Today this part is extremely deteriorated.

88. Garden of the Labyrinth or of the Cross or New

89. Bower of the Lion

Garden of El Cenador or El León

When you walk towards the right, you come to another rectangular area known as the Garden of *El Cenador* because of the beautiful cubic bower renovated in the times of the Emperor (1543-1546) and designed for resting and contemplation (plate 89).

It is surrounded by some galleries with semi-circular arches resting on marble columns bordering on masonry benches with a skirting of glazed tiles.

90. *Carlos V's* bower

The whole cubic centre is also covered inside and outside with valuable glazed tiles executed by the Polido brothers in their Triana ceramic workshops. Above the high skirtings there is Mudéjar plaster work outside and other work of Plateresque design inside.

The ceiling is a superb caissoned dome. Also outstanding is the magnificent flooring which includes the name of Juan Hernández, the architect who executed the works, as well as the date when they were concluded. Attention also should be given to the ground plan of the labyrinth, which may be that existing in the *Alcázar* itself in the 16C.

This garden was also known as that of *El León* because of the lion at the pool and the bower behind it. This pavilion (plate 90), executed in the 17C probably by Diego Martín Orejuela, is one of the most beautiful examples of Mannerism in Seville and originally it was all painted with frescoes inside and outside.

In one of the walls of this garden bounded by the Gallery of *El Grutesco*, there is the beautiful *Puerta del Privilegio*, a door leading to the New Gardens. Parallel to the garden that has just been described there is today's Garden of the Labyrinth, arranged in a modern fashion, but partly imitating the original.

91. Garden of the Poets

Jardines Nuevos

In the area where the orchards beyond the Almohad curtain walls of the *Alcázar* used to be and where the so-called *Huerta del Parque*, later also called *Retiro*, existed in the 17C, today's *Jardines Nuevos* (= New Gardens) were built at the beginning of the century. They were begun by the Marquess of La Vega Inclán and continued by Gómez Millán until 1915, following an aesthetic conception called *Seville garden*, which was a mixture of the elements of the old Renaissance garden, to which fountains and pools of Granada inspiration, glazed tiles, large trees, etc, were added. There is also a section organized along the lines of an English garden and another of Romantic design. In this large area especially noteworthy is the so-called Garden of the Poets, which centres on a large pool and has boundaries consisting of myrtle hedges (plate 91).

This sector of the gardens is therefore bounded by the modern wall built along San Fernando St and the *Paseo de Catalina de Ribera* as well as by the Almohad wall of the *Alcázar* itself, which in the 17C was turned into the Gallery of *El Grutesco* on the façade facing the old gardens. On the side facing the New Gardens, the Marquess of La Vega Inclán built galleries attached to it and near the Tower of *El Enlace* he assembled a beautiful Gothic-Isabelline gate from the Palace of the Dukes of Arcos de Marchena (plate 92). This door or gate leads to the last stage of the itinerary recommended at the beginning.

92. *Puerta de Marchena*

93. A scene in the Garden of *El Chorrón*.
A painting by García y Rodríguez.

94. Garden of *La Alcobilla*

---

(10) In Andalusia, a grille at the end of the entrance hall
(= *zaguán*), closing off the *patio*, but allowing a view of
the flowers, plants and decoration inside.

95. A door with a coat of arms facing the *Apeadero*

In this sector, between the curtain wall and the buildings of the Palace, there are two gardens today, one of them known as the Garden of the China Pavilion and the other as the *Patio del Tenis*. This whole part has been extensively renovated. In the 16C there were several gardens with the following names: *Jardín Alto* or *del Chorrón* (plate 93), which bordered on that of *El Estanque, Jardín del Cidral* in front of the *Cuarto del Cidral, Jardín de la Alcobilla* (plate 94) behind the *Cuarto del Sol* or *del Alcaide* and the *Jardín del Conde* in the area facing that suite.

Today the first garden section is separated from the second by the China Pavilion built in the 18C and 19C and recently restored. It has a *cancela*[10] and grilles dating from the 18C, ie from the time when King Felipe V and his Court stayed at the *Alcázar* in Seville. In fact, his coat of arms in ceramics is adorning the neighbouring portal leading to a roofed passage parallel to the gardens and giving access to the *Apeadero* (plate 95).

The centre of the second garden has a beautiful 16C marble fountain which comes from the Palace of the Dukes of Medina Sidonia. Concealing the curtain wall, old lemon and orange trees are found everywhere in this sector, together with other, recently sown, species. The galleries facing the last mentioned garden belong to the *Cuarto del Sol*, which used to be the residence of the *Alcaide*, or governor, of the *Alcázar*.

96. *Apeadero*

Apeadero[11]

It is a large hall leading to the exit of the *Alcázar* by way of the *Patio de Banderas*. This huge area was restructured at the beginning of the 17C (1607-1609) by the Milanese architect Vermondo Resta, who was the *Maestro Mayor de obras* of the Palace in that period. He built the sumptuous and solemn entrance which almost has the air of a basilica: a nave and two aisles of the same height, the one in the middle being the broadest, with rhythmic semi-circular arches resting on double marble columns of the Tuscan order faced by pilasters supporting arches set in the wall. Beautiful mouldings of the Mannerist kind decorate the spandrels and faces of these arches (plate 96).

This large area contains the doors giving access to the old *Cuarto del Sol* on the left-hand flank and to the *Cuarto del Maestre* on the right, where the offices of the *Alcázar* are today. At the back there is the beginning of the passage which is used when you come from the garden and it is also the beginning of the passage that will take you to the *Patio de la Montería*.

Above the *Apeadero* there was originally an upper hall which, during Felipe V's reign in the 18C, was converted into the Royal Armoury. The fresco decoration of the ceiling still shows the heraldic emblem of the monarch and his wife Doña Isabel de Farnesio. Today it tends to be used as an exhibition gallery and its entrance lies in the right-hand flank of the *Apeadero*.

This hall has a very sumptuous portal facing the *Patio de Banderas*. It was designed by the architect Vermondo Resta and executed by the stone mason Diego Carballo who thus left one of the Mannerist masterpieces in Seville architecture (plate 97). In the central area above the entrance there is a marble plaque with the following inscription:

Reigning in Spain Philippe
the third, this building was raised
in the year MDCVII being repaired
enlarged and converted into the Royal
Armoury in the reign of Philippe V
in the year MDCCXXIX

Under a large wrought-iron crown at the top of the façade there is Felipe V's coat of arms executed in ceramics and at its foot there is another glazed tile with the date of the most recent renovation.

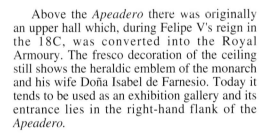

97. Portal of the *Apeadero*

Patio de Banderas (plate 98)

The name comes from the cluster of flags which has always decorated the palace façade on one of the sides of the *patio*. This small fortified enclosure was the parade ground of the original centre of the *Alcázar* and was known by the name of *Dar al-Imara*. At the wall in the back, where the *Apeadero* has its façade, there is the beginning of the passage in the left-hand corner leading to the *Judería* (= Jewish area) and the *Callejón del Agua*. This *patio* is surrounded by houses that used to be the residence of the civil servants in the *Alcázar* in other times. It used to be the place where the recognition ceremonies of the new Spanish monarchs were held by the city of Seville. On such occasions light and fire were used for the celebrations. From this point the view of the Cathedral and its tower, *La Giralda*, is exceptionally beautiful.

98. *Patio de Banderas*

INDEX

GENERAL PLAN OF THE REALES ALCAZARES AND THE GARDENS

1. *Patio de Banderas.*
2. Housing belonging to the Spanish National Trust.
3. *Patio del León* and *Patio de la Montería.*
4. Former Palace of Al-Muwarak.
5. *Patio de los Levíes* and *Patio del Almirante.* Former *Corral de las Piedras.*
6. Suite of *El Almirante* and Hall of Audiences as well as the Chapel of *La Casa de Contratación.*
7. King Don Pedro's Palace.
8. Suite of *El Yeso.*
9. Hall of Justice or the Council.
10. Management and Administration.
11. *Patio* and Garden of the Crossing or of *Doña María de Padilla.*
12. Carlos V's Halls. Former Gothic Palace and Halls of the Vaults and Celebrations.
13. Suite of the Sun or *El Alcaide.*
14. *Apeadero.*
15. Offices of the Spanish National Trust.
16. Tennis Court. Former Garden of *La Alcobilla.*
17. Offices.
18. Offices.
19. Tennis Court.
20. Garden of the Chinese Pavilion.
21. Garden of *El Estanque* (= the Pool).
22. Garden of *La Danza* (= the Dance).
23. Garden of the Labyrinth or of Troy.
24. Garden of the Galley or Galleys.
25. Garden of the Old Grotto.
26. Garden of the Prince.
27. Garden of *Las Damas* (= the Ladies).
28. Garden of the Labyrinth.
29. Garden of the Bower.
30. Carlos V's Bower.
31. Kitchen Garden of *La Alcoba* (= the Bedroom).
32. New Gardens. Former Kitchen Garden of the Park or of the Retreat.
33. Wall of the Dar-al-Imara (913-914).
34. Almohad Wall.
35. *El León* Gate.
36. Gate of the *Patio de Banderas.*
37. Marchena Gate.
38. Gate of the Former Dar-al-Imara.
39. *El Privilegio* Gate.